T0156675

UNDER THE WINGS OF THE LORD ALMIGHTY

Fatimata Gaba Ouedraogo and
Kwawu Mensan Gaba

WESTBOW
P R E S S
A DIVISION OF THOMAS NELSON
& ZONDERVAN

Scripture taken from the Holy Bible, NEW INTERNATIONAL VERSION®. Copyright © 1973, 1978, 1984 by Biblica, Inc. All rights reserved worldwide. Used by permission. NEW INTERNATIONAL VERSION® and NIV® are registered trademarks of Biblica, Inc. Use of either trademark for the offering of goods or services requires the prior written consent of Biblica US, Inc.

WestBow Press books may be ordered through booksellers or by contacting:

WestBow Press
A Division of Thomas Nelson & Zondervan
1663 Liberty Drive
Bloomington, IN 47403
www.westbowpress.com
1 (866) 928-1240

Because of the dynamic nature of the Internet, any web addresses or links contained in this book may have changed since publication and may no longer be valid. The views expressed in this work are solely those of the author and do not necessarily reflect the views of the publisher, and the publisher hereby disclaims any responsibility for them.

Any people depicted in stock imagery provided by Thinkstock are models, and such images are being used for illustrative purposes only. Certain stock imagery © Thinkstock.

ISBN: 978-1-4908-6712-0 (sc)
ISBN: 978-1-4908-6711-3 (hc)
ISBN: 978-1-4908-6710-6 (e)

Library of Congress Control Number: 2015900792

Print information available on the last page.

WestBow Press rev. date: 03/05/2015

CONTENTS

"He will cover you with his feathers,
And under his wings you will find refuge;
His faithfulness will be your shield and rampart" (Psalm 91:4)

". . . how often I have longed to gather your children together, as a hen gathers
her chicks under her wings . . ." (Matthew 23:37)

DEDICATION

To Michael and Fidelia, our beloved children. May you draw inspiration from our family's Indian experience and remain under the wings of the Lord Almighty God all your life.

To all those who are puzzled by their life circumstances. May these pages encourage you to seek the Lord Jesus Christ and reach for the hand of freedom and shelter, which God offers.

ACKNOWLEDGEMENTS

First and foremost, we would like to thank our Lord and Savior Jesus Christ of Nazareth, the author and finisher of our faith, who laid down the path of eternal life and walked on it before us.

We cannot thank our parents, brothers, sisters and friends around the world enough for their continued support and encouragements. They were concerned for us, shared our burdens along the way, and were faithful to pray for us when times got rough.

PREFACE

Even though we were going through difficult times in India, we continued to experience God's grace, deliverance, and an amazing sense of His love in our daily lives. It struck us that the Lord Jesus Christ was calling us to share our story to give Him glory, and to show that He is the Almighty One who never leaves nor forsakes His children as He promised in Hebrews 13:5. We got a firsthand daily demonstration of Jesus' words to His disciples in Luke 12:6–7: "Are not five sparrows sold for two pennies? And yet not one of them is forgotten or uncared for in the presence of God. But even the very hairs of your head are all numbered. Do not be struck with fear or seized with alarm; you are of greater worth than many flocks of sparrows." On many occasions, we've shared pieces of our story, but we were not relieved from the burning sense that we had not fully submitted to the Lord's will. We struggled, procrastinated, and prayed, and finally the Lord opened our eyes to His message of love for humanity everywhere, as He told His disciples James and John "For the Son of Man did not come to destroy men's lives, but to save them." (Luke 9:56, KJV)

We will probably never know why the Lord chose to take us through a rollercoaster to lead us to this place of rest in Him, but did He not send His disciples to the extremities of the world to bear witness to His name (Matthew 28:18)?

We moved from West Africa more than fifteen years ago to the United States, then to India, then back to the United States, and the Almighty God led us to pick up the baton of many of the witnesses He sent before us to continue our sisters and brethren's work under His leadership and care. We were bent but did not break; we were forsaken by man but lifted up by the Almighty God; our enemies set traps, but we did not fall into them; tongues were raised against us but they were silenced; our hearts were broken but we were comforted by God, the one who reigns forever. Our prayer is that at the end of the book you, our beloved reader, will realize that God is so concerned about your eternal life that He uses every detail of your life on earth to lead you to Him.

We tried to recall our experiences, as accurately as possible, and we trust that in His grace, the Lord Jesus Christ will highlight every important detail. We will always remain grateful that the Lord has covered us under His wings, and we pray that you will also be sheltered by Him and find peace in Him. Amen.

In God's love,

Fatimata Gaba Ouedraogo and Kwawu Mensan Gaba

CHAPTER ONE

GOING OUT OF OUR "COMFORT ZONE"

Fatimata

It was hard to understand why we wanted to leave the United States and move to India, because everything was working against it! What a strange idea to uproot the family of four from one country to another. When people asked where we were moving, I said, "To India!" Some of my friends thought it was a terrible idea, to say the least. After the initial reaction, the next set of questions centered on the well-known caste system, and the pollution and congestion problems in India. The latter issues were the major deterrent factor, which everyone close to the family pointed out to us. My doctor clearly advised us against going to live in New Delhi, even if it was only for a three-year professional assignment, because of my problematic health conditions. He gave several examples of people with similar conditions who were unable to sustain the rough Indian environment, but we did not waver in our decision to leave, because we had been led by the Holy Spirit to believe that it was part of our earthly journey.

Why was it so difficult to consider moving to New Delhi?

Breathing regularly is not easy for me. One day, when I was sixteen years old, I was caught by surprise. I was sitting on the porch of our house in Burkina Faso in West Africa when I discovered that breathing wasn't that simple for me! How did it happen? Was it a deterioration of my lungs caused by a lingering cough I was nursing with honey-flavored tea? I didn't know. I just realized that something was wrong with me, and I couldn't breathe!

My brothers and sisters, who witnessed this horrible turning point in my life, could not fathom that I was about to be thrown into a never-ending hurricane of sicknesses. It took a couple of days before one of my uncles, who was in the medical field, suggested that I had "asthma" when I described my symptoms. Back in 1986, with no known family history of asthma, who could have thought of such a disease? Unfortunately, it was not a normal series of asthma attacks. I was administered all the medications known to my limited circle of doctors at the time, but I did not experience any relief from the horrid disease. Every day led to a slow but sure deterioration in my health, as my sickness consumed my body. I would cough for hours at a time, have asthma attacks, and end up exhausted just to restart another tiring episode. Being the oldest of five daughters, the thought running through the family was that people who wanted to destroy our family were spiritually attacking me. Was it true? I didn't know. But one thing was certain: I was gradually losing energy and strength.

Since I could not lie down without coughing, I could not sleep deeply enough to rest and recover from my ailments. I would lay in a very unstable position on a chair, and moving ever so slightly would trigger yet another intense fit of coughing. I could not eat properly because a full stomach would render its contents whenever I started coughing. One of the worst aspects of my sickness was the fact that I became violently allergic to many of my favorite foods, such as pineapple and mango, but I also became allergic to many other beneficial things. In particular, a small product called aspirin. My allergy to aspirin was discovered four months later when I inadvertently took medication

2

that contained aspirin for my menstrual pains, and it triggered a violent asthma attack, for which my father and mother had to rush me to the intensive care unit of the only hospital in town where I'd spent the next ten days recovering. My father was trying to keep his calm; however, one could sense how unsettled and tense he was. He was a man of action, but he could not figure out what to do to battle my disease.

With modern medicine failing to control my asthma, or offering very little improvement for too short a time, many well-intentioned people started advising my parents about alternative medicine or treatments. My father did not have an inclination to follow this advice, but his daughter was suffering. Having exhausted all the modern avenues, my mother just wanted to find a cure for this bizarre disease.

I was launched into the dark world of traditional "doctors." Many of them were just crooks abusing my parents' ignorance and despair. Because of their legitimate desire to see me recover and be healed from my "strange asthma," my parents spent a lot of money on supposed "miracle treatments" based on awkward explanations of the root cause of my problems. They did what any loving parents would have done; they even sold some of their properties to pay for my treatments. Whenever they heard about a "credible" traditional doctor, my parents would take me there, and my mother would stand by my side with the hope that something good would eventually happen. I ended up going from one traditional doctor to another, consuming all kinds of beverages and mixtures, sometimes made of repulsive and quite sickening ingredients, like goat's poop or fungus, which could have killed me with their high toxicity.

None of these doctors was able to provide a cure to my disease, and my problem was getting worse. My father faithfully drove me to various appointments, but my mother was the most impacted by our situation. She would stay with me throughout these long examinations, and my disease started to take a toll on her health too, as she watched me "die slowly." My brothers and sisters were trying their best to encourage me, but everyone was under stress. Eventually, my sickness brought me to the point where I weighed less than twenty-five kilograms (fifty-five pounds) for a height of 165 centimeters (about five foot seven). All it took was one glance to see that something was seriously wrong. At sixteen years old, my bones were jutting out of my skin, and I had rings under my eyes. In the midst of my struggle, some close family members had told my mother to get ready for my burial thinking I would not make it, but she refused to give up on me, and refused to let me succumb to my disease. Finding a cure was a costly race against time, and there was no respite for my parents. How could they let this horrible disease take away the life of their firstborn daughter?

It was so easy to fall prey to traditional doctors, because everyone was operating in ignorance. At that time in Burkina Faso, the health system was not developed and many people were still dying from illnesses such as diarrhea and other well-contained diseases such as typhoid, malaria, yellow fever, etc. The traditional doctors were just taking advantage of my situation and my parents' distress. If my parents did not have any means to seek treatment, I would have been left alone to suffer after all the unsuccessful and costly trials. But they were hopeful that somehow in this large crowd of swindlers, a small sliver of hope could be found.

My Muslim parents also heeded the advice of taking me to prayer meetings in various churches including Assemblies of God churches, because they were told that God performed miracles there, and they had heard about people being delivered from all kinds of afflictions. Every evening, my mother and I went to an evangelical crusade led by well-known Evangelist Reinhart Bonnke. Several people came forward to give testimonies about their healing, and I witnessed some amazing things, but nothing miraculous happened to me. My mother and I met with pastors and they prayed for me, but I was not healed. I went to these churches without faith, but even though I was skeptical about the help I could get, I continued to go because I did not want to discourage my mother. She was really desperate for me. Every time we saw another pastor or visited another church, she literally begged me to have faith and believed that I would be healed! Obviously, she and I didn't know that according to the book of Hebrews, "Faith is being sure of what we hope for and certain of what we do not see," and that "without faith it is impossible to please God, because anyone who comes to Him must believe that He exists and that He rewards those who earnestly seek Him" (Hebrews 11:1, 6). Even though I wanted badly to be healed, nothing positive came out of the prayer sessions.

As my disease progressed, new symptoms were discovered. I was diagnosed with severe sinusitis, for which I had to travel to Côte d'Ivoire, a neighboring country for treatment. The trip by train was a long one (more than twelve hours), and I undertook it while having a high fever. My mother was desperately worried, not knowing if I would even make it, but by the grace of God, we safely arrived in Abidjan, the capital city of Côte d'Ivoire, where I received adequate treatment.

My academic life was obviously compromised, as I was too weak most of the time to study. My mother always encouraged me to persevere, and I eventually developed quite an efficient system of studying. Whenever I had a little window of proper breathing with the slightest bit of relief from coughing, I quickly learned the academic materials I had because I did not know what would happen next. Quite often, my parents drove me to school to take the exams right after several

5

asthma attacks, but even my strong will to succeed was not enough to make it through some of the critical exams. I had to take the general certificate "A" level exam three times because of my illness, although I was among the top three students all of those years. Nobody could say if I would ever go to college.

By the end of the first two years since the beginning of my illness, the disease had already fully manifested itself through its typical symptoms—severe daily coughing, daily asthma attacks, sinusitis due to nasal polyps, and an allergy to aspirin, but no medical professional was able to connect the dots and make the proper diagnostic. The doctors still couldn't put a definite name on my condition.

With all these conventional asthma treatments not providing the expected results, I was introduced to corticosteroids, which would provide temporary relief. The use of corticosteroids was supposed to be for a short period of time, and for emergency purposes only, but it was the only medication that could help me cope with my symptoms. From fortnightly doses administered through intramuscular injections, I quickly moved to weekly doses using the same procedures, then to daily oral doses because of the high risks of affecting my muscles, bones, and overall mental and emotional being. Gradually, the daily doses were increased to produce the same effects as before. High corticosteroids[1] became my asthma controller and painkiller, or so I believed, and I was addicted. By early 1990, almost four years after the onset of this "bizarre" disease, I was taking a heavy dose of corticosteroids (often up to 60 mg a day for long periods) to control

---

[1] Corticosteroids have well-known side effects. When taking oral corticosteroids on a long-term basis, you could experience: (i) clouding of the lens in one or both eyes (cataracts), (ii) high blood sugar, which can trigger or worsen diabetes, (iii) increased risk of infections, (iv) thinning bones (osteoporosis) and fractures, (iv) suppressed adrenal gland hormone production, and (vi) thin skin, easy bruising, and slower wound healing.

or stabilize my situation. Immediately after the start of my treatment, I noticed the side effects of the corticoids—puffy face and high water retention—but I was not too worried at the time because I was young and wanted relief from my pain and suffering to pursue my dreams. The price to pay to have a pseudo-normal life was high, but I hoped that a cure for my disease would be found early enough for me to stop taking those medications. The medications were considerably weakening my immune system, and according to doctors, they were bound to destroy my body and mind.

CHAPTER TWO

FROM DARKNESS TO LIGHT

Fatimata

Two events in 1990 changed the dynamics of my situation. First, I placed second in the competitive entrance exam to a renowned college in Côte d'Ivoire, West Africa—the Interafrican Electrical Engineering College (IEEC)—which automatically granted me a full scholarship[2] sponsored by the electricity utility of my country, and, on top of that achievement, I was the only female among the five selected candidates. Only high school seniors with majors in mathematics and physics who have consistently ranked among the top three students throughout the year, if not through high school,[3] were eligible to take the exam. And, even after selection, entrance to the college was determined on another exam open to all seniors, which I completed. In the midst of my condition, I saw this as a blessing from God, who was also providing financial relief and hope to my exhausted parents. Close relatives came to talk my parents out of the decision to let me go to college. According to them, my

---

[2] In addition to the full scholarship, the sponsor company provided to the student upon graduation a full time engineer job for at least ten years.

[3] In Burkina Faso's educational system, middle school has four years and high school has three years. Right after middle school, students are directed to three main sections: one with major in humanities, one with major in natural sciences, and one with major in mathematics and physics. The last section was considered the toughest and most selective one, and as a result, has fewer students.

poor health would not allow me to sustain the rigorous academic and physical regimen of the five-year curriculum.[4] But little did they know that everything was being orchestrated by the Lord Almighty. Nothing and no one could deter my parents, who fully knew the risks, and agreed to let me travel on my own to Bingerville, Côte d'Ivoire, where the Lord was leading me.

At twenty one year old, I was finally entering college when all my close friends were getting ready to graduate. I was looking forward to the new phase in my life but I was still full of apprehension because of my poor health.

I started the academic year in early September 1990. The first few weeks were difficult to handle, as I was having regular asthma attacks and could not attend classes. I was physically drained at night, and all I could do was sleep after enduring the eight hours of lecturing each day. I cried a lot in the isolation of my room. I missed my mother, her whole-hearted support, and the comfort of my family home. Who could provide assistance in this cold, competitive, and predominantly male environment? I didn't know. The other woman in my cohort was an easygoing native of Côte d'Ivoire. We became good friends, but I could not rely on her or on any other person completely, because my condition was so difficult to manage.

My parents called as regularly as possible, but they could not spend the whole day on the phone. Even if they could, they would not have been able to help me. I was in Côte d'Ivoire, another country,

---

[4] Each academic year of the five-year program was divided into a nine-month theoretical training at the college campus followed by a two-month practical training in the sponsoring organization to help acquaint students to the requirements of their future professional life. After the eleven-month period, students were given a month vacation before returning to the school for the following year.

and they were in Burkina Faso, a three-hour flight away. My mother always encouraged me not to give up, but the transition was very hard.

After a month, the entire student population came back from summer vacation, and the two other female students of the school who were from Côte d'Ivoire and Congo also resumed classes. Because they were in the third and fifth years and of my age group, I could mingle more easily with them, and this began to ease my feelings of helplessness. Since they had already gone through the first year, they gave me useful advice about the courses as well as tips on faculty's teaching styles. These female students gave me pertinent guidance and helped me in ways I could not imagine. Later on, I found out they were Christians.

Meeting a group of Christians was the other turning point in my ordeal. I had heard many things about Christians at the college, but I was interested in a particular group based on how they expressed their faith. They talked about Christ in a very forceful way, and their message was essentially to repent from sin, turn to Jesus Christ, as He is the only way to God and the assurance to escape from hell. According to the Bible, they said, everyone was a sinner and good works or deeds couldn't save anyone no matter how hard you tried or were successful! This was contrary to what I was accustomed to given my Muslim background. According to Romans 3:23, all humans are bound to death, "for all have sinned and fall short of the glory of God." But God in His love has prepared a plan and sent His only begotten son, Jesus Christ of Nazareth, born out of a virgin. Through Jesus Christ only, humans can have the free gift of salvation. "For the wages of sin is death, but the gift of God is eternal life in Christ Jesus our Lord" (Romans 6:23). For that reason, if we do not accept Jesus Christ as our Lord and Savior, and die in our sins, we will go to hell for eternity.

Not many among the bright and successful students at the college wanted to hear that message, since they associated Christianity with a boring religion that would not allow them to enjoy life. It was also the first time that I had been fully exposed to it. Was all that important? My visits to prayer meetings in the past were to seek healing and not the Lord Jesus Christ. I was not a bad person, and even though I was sick, I was trying to handle my own life and not be a burden to others. Could it be possible that I came to Bingerville for something more than my engineering studies? I was trying to avoid thinking about the message but it was clear. What would be the reaction of the schoolmates who warned me about those called Christians trying to convert everybody to Christianity? They always made fun of Christians. I was struggling with these questions, but I had to recognize that some of the members of the group were very caring. They would pray for me when I had my asthma attacks. They would bring me along when they were going to the capital city for errands, take me out to dinner, or accompany me to my doctors' appointment whenever possible. They treated me with thoughtfulness, and encouraged me to persevere in my studies. I felt safe in their company. But they always talked to me about how Jesus Christ loved me and died for my sins. I experienced the love of Christ through the compassion shown to me by members of that group, and I came to realize how much God loved me. I gave my life to the Lord Jesus Christ and personally asked Him to be my shepherd for eternity, basing my faith on Romans 10:9–10, "If you declare with your mouth, 'Jesus is Lord,' and believe in your heart that God raised him from the dead, you will be saved. For it is with your heart that you believe and are justified, and it is with your mouth that you profess your faith and are saved." For the first time since I fell sick, I was no longer afraid of my disease!

I then informed my Muslim parents that I had become a Christian, and they did not oppose it. They even gave me their blessings, saying that if I could find relief in Christ, then they would also be relieved. What a surprising outcome that my Muslim parents would bless me for becoming a Christian![5]

As I discovered later on, many of the members of the group were members or regular attendees of the Assemblies of God church, and they strongly believed in divine healing. After I explained all the side effects of my medication and my unstable health situation despite the high doses of corticosteroids, they were convinced that my acceptance of Jesus Christ as my Lord and Savior was the beginning of my body's healing process. They believed that through prayer and fasting the Lord Jesus Christ would intervene and grant me freedom because He came to give life, and life in abundance, to those who follow Him (Isaiah 53:4–5; John 10:8–10). We prayed for my healing, and I even tried to fast for one day, but I realized that I was not prepared to embark upon such experience. I was more focused on the transformation that was taking place in my mind and in my emotions. The joy of the Lord filled my heart and the feeling of being helpless disappeared. I just knew deep inside me that God was now taking care of me. When I looked back through all through the dark periods of my life, I saw that God was leading me to Him. He did not allow all these medications to kill me. In fact, He had performed the greatest miracle of all—He saved my life and gave me hope.

All these events took place in a span of four months after I started college. In December 1990, after I had accepted Jesus Christ as my Lord and Savior I did have asthma attacks, but I noticed some changes in my overall health. I continued to take my corticosteroids as prescribed, but now I had peace of mind that God would take care of the side effects. I was now "stable," and I knew that my

---

[5] Several Muslims who became Christians faced a lot of persecutions. Some were rejected by their families as apostates.

medications were no longer the absolute anchor for my survival. I was safe in God's hands.

On the academic front, positive things started happening. The long, intense school days I was so afraid of became bearable, and I was able to have a fairly normal student life. Against previous expectations, I did complete the first year of university and was promoted to the second year. My family was extremely proud of me, and I knew that I solely owed it to the Lord's grace. This unexpected success happened every subsequent year. At the end of the school year, I would go back to my country for my summer internship and vacation, and in September, I would come back to school, trusting the Lord would again sustain me throughout the new academic year. I regularly attended church services and bible study groups on campus, and I successfully completed the course requirements for graduation. I did my Master of Science thesis research on the conversion of pumps into turbines for the dual purpose of irrigation and power generation. Finally, in June 1995, I graduated as the first female electromechanical engineer of Burkina Faso. Although the five-year regimen was rigorous, I completed it by God's grace without repeating a year. He was able to complete the work He had started in my academic life (Philippians 1:6).

CHAPTER THREE

FINDING AN IMPOSSIBLE LOVE AND EXPECTING TO MARRY ONE DAY

Fatimata

As educators, my parents always wanted each of their five daughters to achieve academic success and not to depend on our three older brothers. They raised us with the motto that "a woman's work should be likened to a husband." In our traditional Burkinabe society, past a certain age, the woman was to marry and raise a family. In addition, coming from a royal family[6], I received a strict moral education with repeated warnings about relationships with men as princesses were expected to practice sexual abstinence. If they got pregnant out of wedlock, they were banned from the village. They could not even entertain any relationship with their family wherever they were. I remember how the preferred daughter of my uncle who was also a princess was banned from the village after she got pregnant. Her father initially resisted the ban, but diseases and death started to unfold in the family and my uncle had to let her go. This environment made me hold on to my parents' motto tightly. My mother and I used to discuss how banning pregnant girls was a cruel practice, as the girls were chased away and abandoned when they most needed help. But there was no other alternative. In the village,

---

[6] My grandfather was the king of a village.

everyone was subject to this rule, strictly enforced by the elders and the "spirits" of the village. Since I was the firstborn daughter, my parents were especially watchful because they did not want to go through any such experience. When my sickness started, this became of a lesser concern. When I left for my engineering studies, these issues came back again to mind. However, I noticed that I had developed a natural protection mechanism, a strong repulsion for any boy who could have been attracted to me because I would see him as a potential threat or cause for ban.

This repulsion melted away when I became a Christian. I realized that God loved me and I did not have to live in fear. Didn't the Apostle Paul declare in 2 Timothy 1:7, "For God has not given us a spirit of fear, but of power and of love and of a sound mind"? It also dawned on me that the people in my village were trying to enforce sexual abstinence by their own means and for the wrong motive, the pride of the throne. In 1 Corinthians 6:9–11, the Apostle Paul gave a stark warning and a clear explanation that holiness proceeds from our relationship with God:

> Do you not know that the wicked will not inherit the kingdom of God? Do not be deceived: Neither the sexual immoral nor idolaters nor adulterers nor male prostitutes nor homosexual offenders nor thieves nor the greedy nor drunkards nor slanderers nor swindlers will inherit the kingdom of God. As that is what some of you were. But you were washed, you were sanctified, you were justified in the name of the Lord Jesus Christ and by the Spirit of our God.

As I was growing in my new relationship with the Lord Jesus Christ, my interactions within the group of believers grew. I fell in love with

Kwawu a fifth-year Christian student toward the end of my first year in college.

Kwawu was a dreamer and fascinated by scientific research and how it could help address great challenges in the world. As he was in his final year, his mind was on pursuing further studies in electrical engineering. He viewed my being a freshman in 1991 as an opportunity for him to focus on his projects rather than making marriage plans, which we could not fulfill anyway.

Being in an evangelical community, both of us understood and were practicing the teachings of 1 Corinthians 6:18–20: "Flee from sexual immorality. All other sins a man commits are outside his body, but he who sins sexually sins against his own body. Do you not know that your body is the temple of the Holy Spirit, who is in you, whom you have received from God? You are not your own; you were bought at a price. Therefore honor God with your body."

We trusted God to keep us pure until our marriage and despite a lot of opposition from his family, we decided in July 1991 with the guidance of the Holy Spirit to pledge or commit to marry each other at God's appointed time. We were engaged before the Lord Jesus Christ but did not know how this whole relationship could work, me having the obligations to fulfill a ten-year contract with my sponsor company and him the same. Only the trust in the Word of God made us stand firm with our relationship.

When he graduated in July 1991, he went back to his country Togo to work at the national electricity utility with the open ambition to undertake further studies as soon as the Lord opened a door for him. Between 1991 and 1994, when he left Togo for Canada, we met in Ivory Coast, where I was still in college, a couple of times and in Burkina Faso in August 1993 where he came with his mother and brother to meet my family. Although the encounter between our two families marked a step toward our wedding, it was simply not enough to assuage my concerns. Kwawu was still living in his dreams, as focused as ever on his ambitions.

Knowing my medical condition, my friends were repeatedly advising me to quickly marry to avoid the potential problem of me not being able to conceive because of the long-term corticotherapy. Whenever the question was raised in Kwawu's presence, his response was invariably the same: "God will provide: Mary got pregnant while she was a virgin, and Sarah got pregnant at an old age. When Fatimata and I eventually marry, she will be between those two extreme situations. So there is no need to worry!"

After my graduation in July 1995, I returned to Burkina Faso and started working at the national electricity utility, as provided for under the scholarship agreement. I was able to distinguish myself as a competent power engineer, working on electrification projects. However, I was again confronted with the dusty environment, and this triggered my allergies and breathing difficulties. As noted before, one of the major side effects of the corticosteroids is the toll on the immune system, rendering it weaker and weaker, making my body prone to infections. Whenever I had an infection, in addition to taking antibiotics, I had to increase my daily dose of corticoids to help my body fight the germs. I had already been on corticoids for about nine years by then and there were no alternative in sight. Another major effect was the risk of irreversible alteration of my ability to conceive and the reduction of bone density, which concerned my family and me. How would I cope with all this in the long run? If I wanted to reduce my daily doses, the coughing and asthma attacks would get out of control.

Now that I had a stable job with good benefits, everyone in the family started wondering what would come next. My colleagues always asked about Kwawu, who had left Togo at the end of 1994 to pursue further studies in electrical engineering in Montreal, Canada. But I could not talk about our future plans since I did not have any clue myself. Toward the end of January 1996, he called to tell me that he was leaving again Montreal to go to Quebec City. I thought it was suspicious because he did not want to give me much information over the phone. A couple of months later, he told me that he was leaving Quebec City and was heading to Washington, DC. What was going on with him?

Sometimes, I doubted his sincerity and wondered if he was a serious man who would stabilize one day, but my mother was his biggest supporter. She would watch over me as if she was from his family. I even asked him if we should end this difficult relationship. His family was so opposed to our relationship because I was sick, and they anticipated he would suffer. His mother and brother, both in the medical field and well aware of the side effects of corticosteroids, were not a big help. My fiancé would always remind me about the one who led us to be together, the Lord Jesus Christ, and reiterated that we only had to look up to Him for our relationship. When he was in DC, we had more frequent phone interactions and the discussions about marriage became real. In July 1996, he finally conveyed that he was ready for marriage, citing a conviction from the Lord. After so many years, he finally committed to a marriage date and it was set in August 1997, six years after we got engaged.

But since he was so far away, and we had not seen each other for more than two years, we had to do a lot of planning. The first thing we needed to take care of was to secure our parents' consents. Given my royal background, it was impossible for me to marry without my parents' consent, and my parents would not agree without formally meeting his parents. That was a fact of life he had to deal with and he worked on it. His parents came from Lomé, Togo to meet mine in Ouagadougou, Burkina Faso in February 1997 and asked for my hand, which my entire family agreed to give him. Uncles, aunts, and family acquaintances showed up for the big reception my parents organized because everyone wanted to see who "The Togolese's" parents were. It was the first time I was meeting my father-in-law to be, but the third time I met my mother-in-law to be. Since they were from a foreign country, my parents talked to elders in our village to simplify the traditional marriage requirements (the number of visits to the village by the marriage candidate before the actual celebrations). After almost six years, the two families had finally given their consent, which was a great blessing! Considering the road traveled, from Côte d'Ivoire where we met to where we would be coming from for the marriage, it was difficult to imagine that the story had started as improbable because of our differences and was now going to conclude happily. After his parents' visit, our wedding plans started to accelerate.

After several discussions, my parents recommended that all the wedding festivities be celebrated in Togo. We eventually decided that the wedding was to take place in the Temple du Calvaire in Lomé, where he had been a member. By the Lord's grace, my fiancé could now afford the marital expenses, having worked for many months in Washington, DC. To organize the wedding in Lomé, we had to rely on his friends and parents, which proved to be a highly emotional decision.

In April 1997, he had a short professional trip to Lomé and we agreed to meet there. Although we exchanged letters and spoke over the phone regularly, we were surprised to see how much we had both evolved over the past two years. After his trip, he came over to Ouagadougou. I had the pleasure to show him some of the projects I had done as a power engineer in my country since my graduation in 1995. I was also thinking about the nagging question about what would happen after we married. This was a question on everyone's lips, but Kwawu's unwavering answer was that I should move to Washington, DC, with him and start over there. He argued that he had waited for so long not to have his wife with him, and in any case, he did not think we had any other viable options, especially given my health issues. From his perspective, I would have access to a better care system in the US, and I would be taken off my long-term debilitating corticotherapy.

CHAPTER FOUR

DISCOVERING MY HUSBAND AND ADJUSTING TO MY NEW LIFE

Fatimata

On August 16, 1997, we finally celebrated our wedding, and it also happened to be my birthday. The promise of the Lord came to pass. The opposition did not prevail over God's plan for us to get married. Didn't the Bible say "be patient and wait for the deliverance of the Lord"? We were surrounded by family and friends, and several relatives traveled from various countries to attend the wedding ceremony. My husband was extremely happy and his face glowed with happiness. Although I was happy, I could not rejoice as intensely as I would have wanted it. I had several apprehensions about moving to the US. All the attempts to defer my trip to the US were turned down by my husband. He was convinced that the best thing for us was to be together and experience the promise of the Lord in Matthew 18:19 that "Again, truly I tell you that if two of you on earth agree about anything they ask for, it will be done for them by my Father in heaven." My parents wholeheartedly supported him!

After the wedding in Lomé, Togo we traveled back to Ouagadougou, Burkina Faso and took off from there to Washington, DC, via Dakar, Senegal. I now had to learn how to be a wife and work faithfully with my husband. This was not easy, given the time we spent apart, and it was a totally new experience for me to settle in Washington, DC. I was going through a triple transition at the time, from fiancée to wife, from Francophone Burkina Faso to the Anglophone environment in the US, from an active professional with a secure job to a job seeking one. Marriage was supposed to be bliss, but it turned out to be quite tricky to handle. On top of all that, my "special asthma" needed some attention, and I heeded the advice to start working on finding an alternative treatment.

Through the insurance referral system, we got in touch with a pneumologist who had a good professional reputation. He had me try different non-steroid medications, but after all the tests and trials, he confirmed the doses I was taking were adequate to control my asthma. He explained to me the side effects of prednisone (corticoid available in the US) and referred me to one of his colleagues, an endocrinologist, to look after my adrenal glands, which by then, according to several doctors, would have stopped functioning given the high dose of steroids and the long period over which I was taking these medications. The tests confirmed that I have developed a cortico-induced adrenal insufficiency and my pneumologist started me on higher doses of prednisone, much higher than the amount our body normally produces.

Contradicting everyone's expectations, I got pregnant three months after my marriage. This was a miracle, since doctors had little faith in me being able to conceive. Some even advised to abort, claiming that the baby might have significant health issues, as some of the exams showed a high chance of Down syndrome. My obstetric-gynecologist even started preparing us for this eventuality. We again had to go to Jesus, our rock and refuge, for help. The pregnancy was painful, with all-day sickness, and my asthma was not controlled. To help alleviate my pain, the pneumologist increased my daily doses of prednisone above 100 mg. To taper my doses was nowhere on the short-term agenda. I took these high doses until the baby was delivered in July 1998, and after that, the doses were gradually reduced. Because of what I had been through during the pregnancy, the pneumologist was strongly reluctant to further pursue the reduction of my prednisone intakes. My husband and I realized that there was no possible solution in the US! I was stuck with these high doses but happy to be a mother of a cute, healthy boy, Michael.

Doctors were happily surprised with the outcome of the pregnancy and advised against another attempt, saying that the risk would be much higher and it would either be fatal to me or to the baby. Afraid, we agreed that I should take birth control injections but it turned out to be a disaster, as I was constantly bleeding because of hormonal imbalance or interference with the corticotherapy. We didn't factor in God's will for us, so we finally decided that I should stop taking this type of birth control medication and switch to another one. In addition, it was tough to juggle my added responsibilities and my intention to pursue a career, with a husband who was also regularly traveling out of the US for business purposes.

In the summer 1999, my husband was transferred for a two-year stint in Paris (France) and we gladly embraced the move to the City of Lights. Because it was Paris and we had so many friends in France, we did not pay much attention to the local environment problems. Unlike the Washington area, where we were living in a greener environment, Paris proved to have high levels of car pollution. We regularly noticed deposits of dirt on our windows and curtains, and since I had the guidelines for managing my corticoid medications, I would increase the daily dose whenever I felt a discomfort.

I do not know if it was the romantic feel of Paris, but as soon as we arrived, I got pregnant again, although under birth control.

The passion must have been overwhelming! I discovered it the day my son started walking on his own at fourteen months. What a relief, as I was dreading the thought of handling my pregnancy with a baby still dependent. The news was not at all welcomed by my husband. He had to pray to come to grips that it was the plan of the Lord and He, the Almighty God, would conduct it to its term. I was joyful though scared, not knowing what to expect. Fortunately, in Paris, I found a gynecologist who was comfortable prescribing medication to pregnant women with severe morning or rather all-day sickness. I gladly took the medications and was able to eat comfortably. I managed to go through the pregnancy and delivered a beautiful, healthy baby girl in April 2000, named Fidelia, which means, "God is faithful."

Besides the pollution, the day-to-day life in Paris was not as easy as my husband and I anticipated it would be. After the delivery, my respiratory discomfort grew significantly, and the heavy doses of corticosteroids could not overcome it. On several occasions, I had to be rushed to the emergency room of the American Hospital of Paris. By the Lord's grace, we met a pneumologist, who in collaboration with a team of specialists, reviewed my complete medical history and diagnosed that I was suffering from a severe sinusitis that could only be treated by surgery. Through research and perseverance, the doctors were able to pin down the name of the disease I was suffering from, a sickness known as Samter's triad.

According to publicly available information, this condition was first described in 1922 by Widal et al. The article was published in French and largely ignored for the next forty-five years. It wasn't until 1968 when Samter and Beers, two renowned medical doctors, described patients with the symptom triad of asthma, aspirin sensitivity, and nasal polyps that the condition became recognized and known as Samter's triad.

More than twelve years after the onset of the disease, I was finally able to put a name to it. And, according to my pneumologist, only two forms exist: one that can only be controlled by corticosteroids, and one that does not need corticosteroids. Obviously, I had the form that could only be controlled by corticosteroids. All of a sudden, a big light gushed into my heart and mind. I realized that neither I nor my parents had any choice about the treatment. The countless nights and days I spent resisting the intake of corticosteroids were simply adding to my misery. The guilt that my parents carried for having not been able to find an adequate, less-damaging treatment was not justified. It had oppressed them ever since I started my corticosteroids and my mother always explained, with fatalism, that it was the only treatment that worked. For my husband, it was again a demonstration that God was under control! Although it has a lot of side effects, the corticosteroids were still the only option for me! Without them, I would not have lived long enough to know the truth.

My pneumologist went on to say it was simply a miracle that I was able to give birth to two normal children with my condition and long-term corticotherapy, to which everyone in my family and I fully agreed. "Jesus looked at them and said, 'With man this is impossible, but with God all things are possible'" (Matthew 19:26).

He clearly advised me that continuing on the corticosteroids was not a sustainable course. He was astonished that my bone density was fairly normal, after more than twelve years taking such high doses of corticosteroids. My husband and I asked him about what the alternative would be to not taking corticosteroids. The doctor was pretty blunt and said that unless something changed in my treatment, I was bound to a health disaster. Corticosteroids have the dark side effects to create random conditions. After trying to put me back on non-corticosteroid medication for asthma, my pneumologist realized that I was having the same problems as I was in the US. However, he did more research and found a new corticosteroid inhaler that was recently released, and he designed a new treatment protocol for me with the ultimate objective to reduce my oral intake of corticosteroids. His strategy was to have the inhaler compensate for the reduction in my daily dose while I was under medical supervision. He also explained that I should never try to abruptly stop or drop my corticosteroid in a drastic manner because it could create a possibly fatal shock. He also recommended a nutritionist to alter my diet to prevent excessive weight gain, given my body's oscillations between size fourteen and eighteen (the concentration of the weight gain primarily in my abdominal area, back and face). My husband and I found a renewed impetus in the fight against Samter's triad.

During that period of trials, friends, brothers, and sisters in Christ in various countries prayed for us. Regular prayers were given on our behalf in my country. Given the difficult situation and the fact that our children were very young, my mother also overcame her strong reluctance to travel alone from Burkina Faso and came to assist us in Paris for a couple of months. Her arrival was really a blessing, as she was able to take care of her grandchildren and gave me some comfort. In the midst of all these difficulties, God was consistently faithful in watching over us. Didn't He say in Hebrews 13:5 "Never will I leave you; never will I forsake you."

While God was sustaining us through all those health issues and the challenges of raising young children, He even provided professional opportunities beyond my expectations one day at a time. During our stay in Paris, I was able to get a work contract with the French electricity company and also complete in 2001, the coursework for another master degree in Economics, majoring in industrial organization[7].

---

[7] I had to come back to France in 2002 to present my research thesis.

In July 2001, we moved back to the US, and the adjustment process restarted. Now that I had a better understanding of what I was suffering from, my husband and I quickly got in touch with my US pneumologist to review my treatment strategy. Unfortunately, it did not last long before I realized that all the recent progress was quickly erased. Any attempt to reduce the daily dose of prednisone below twenty mg per day proved extremely hard to maintain. Was it because of the stress of running a family in Washington, DC with young children and a traveling husband? I didn't have any emotional break with the children when their father was on the road. My daughter would cry for days, wanting her father, and my son would be sick during most of his absences. My husband and I discussed adjustments to his travel schedule and he finally settled on business trips that would not leave him out of the country for more than two weekends in a row. However, even with that regimen, the situation did not improve that much and we had to find a solution, as I started feeling weak again on a consistent basis.

I was adamant not to stay at these high doses of corticosteroids. We again spoke with my US pneumologist and quickly realized that he would not take the risk to continue the work started in France. Through referral at my husband's office, we got in touch with a renowned allergy specialist. We explained the whole story to him and clearly stated our goal to reduce and even eliminate the oral intake of corticosteroids. Several new products for the treatment of asthma and/or allergies were released in the US, and according to the allergy specialist, patients were recording significant improvements. Although I tried several of these new medications, including expensive monthly shots of an experimental treatment, I did not experience any breakthrough. I could not tell how many times we prayed about this condition and asked God for relief. My husband regularly quoted John 11:39–44, which relates the resurrection of Lazarus. For my husband, if God could restore a decaying body and bring it to life with full functionality, it was not dormant adrenal glands that He could not heal. After a certain period, with regular medical follow-up and the combination of several inhalers, my asthma started to "behave."

I began to make professional plans again and look for job opportunities. At first, it was hard to restart, but gradually, with the Lord's help, I was able to line up interesting consulting contracts relating to the energy sector and enhance my professional edge, building on the technical and economic perspective I had on the energy sector. I told myself that I could now focus on my professional career, and I believed God was setting me on the right path. I had health issues that I was able to deal with, but nothing prepared me for the shock I was about to face. Without warning, I started having violent headaches in 2005. At the same time, I was also having stomach problems. Given my medical history, the attention was focused on the side effects of the corticotherapy. I did all possible sophisticated medical exams but to no avail. Doctors were able to pick up a slight reduction in bone density but nothing could explain my symptoms. I was going from one specialist to the other, and no one was able to look at all the symptoms and exam results in a holistic manner and give a diagnostic. For months, my symptoms looked like the side effects of the corticosteroids, and we were spinning around, with my energy at a very low level. I had all kinds of pains in my body, and my skin felt as if it was an open wound. The doctors were sometimes concerned that I might have something incurable. The situation was so serious that my husband stopped all his business travels to focus on the resolution of my problems. There was no relief at sight.

Again, in His mercy, the Lord Jesus Christ led us through the network of an allergy specialist to get in touch with an experienced medical doctor. After reviewing my history, he ordered additional exams, and he finally concluded that I was suffering from a severe anemia. I had to be given intravenous iron because the tablets I was regularly taking were not working effectively. After a series of inoculation of intravenous iron, my health improved dramatically, but I was really tired of being sick. The endocrinologist checked the residual life of my adrenal glands and the tests showed that they were producing just a small quantity of cortisol, barely noticeable, and certainly not enough to sustain my entire body, which needs to produce at least 7.5 mg per day.

With the emotional toll of the last health crisis, my husband and I decided to go back to the project we started in Paris: getting rid of my high doses of oral corticosteroids. Our return from France had gradually brought us back to our eating and life patterns. My family responsibilities were very demanding and I could not juggle them with my professional ones with such a poor health. There was no way I could manage both without a restored body. This time, I promised myself that I would not stop trying to get rid of the corticosteroids I was taking and again prayed the Lord to sustain me.

I committed myself to taking the medications that were supposed to help control my asthma in the long run and discussed with my internist a protocol to decrease my oral corticosteroids. I went from 20 to 15 mg but had to use my emergency inhaler quite often during the day. When it became difficult, I had to increase to 20 mg or more again before coming down to 15 mg. I spent time reading about Samter's triad to see if there were any new developments. Learning from people's experiences in fasting and praying, I started focusing more on my nutrition/diet, selecting products that would not trigger allergies, and exercising to increase my respiratory capacity and endurance. After a couple of months, I thought I reached a stable situation and I dropped my oral dose to 10 mg but had to take it up again to 15 mg.

I went through lengthy and tiring trials, which could not stabilize my asthma. Since we were praying the Lord Almighty, we were convinced that we had to take bolder steps. I wanted to get rid of the medication that was crippling me. With the combination of the initiatives, I eventually got to a daily dose of 10 mg and could not go lower. The trick in all these trials was to avoid any infection, because if I had an infection, I had to increase my dose three times for about two weeks, decrease it to 20 mg, 15 mg, and then go back to 10 mg. All along my husband and I were praying for my adrenal glands to be quickened, and with the help of my sister who moved into our house, I got some physical relief and good cheer, which helped distract me from my disease. We were stuck at a daily dose of 10 mg, and any combination to lower it further could not work, because my asthma was too unstable. It was in the midst of those difficult trials that we were working on our move to India.

For my allergy doctor, who has witnessed this difficult battle, it was impossible for him to give us the medical clearance to travel to India. It was April 2008 and we were to move that summer. He expressed serious concerns about the move, as I was still unstable and needed a regular follow-up. I myself was not as convinced as my husband about this journey, but I trusted that our Lord who led him would also convince me. Questions flowed through my mind: "How would God tell us to go to India in this already difficult situation? Does He make mistakes?" To which 1 Corinthians 1:25 would respond forcefully that ". . . the foolish thing in God is wiser than men, and the weak thing from God is stronger than men . . ."

CHAPTER FIVE

CAN I AFFORD NOT TO EMBRACE THE WILL OF GOD?

Kwawu

I have been faithfully working for several years as a power engineer in the Africa region of the World Bank. Although not always easy, I very much liked my work. In April 2007, I got an email from a colleague in the human resources department asking me whether I would consider applying for the job of lead energy specialist for India advertised in the South Asia department of the organization. The position was based in New Delhi, India. Someone had circulated that advertisement before in an effort to generate interest, but I mentally disregarded it because, knowing my work environment, it was obvious to me it was one of those earmarked positions that were always hard for black Africans to get because of stereotyping and unfairness. In disbelief, I read the email again and closed my computer. It was Easter break, and I chose to focus my mind on more important things. I wanted to reflect on the atonement work by the Lord Jesus Christ.

A couple of days later, I went to see my colleague and asked him repeatedly whether this was a strategy to use me as a "sparring partner" to validate the selection of a preferred candidate. There have been many instances where black Africans were entered in a competition for this sole purpose. Since he could not provide much detail, he advised me to call his colleague in charge of the recruitment process and find out by myself.

I called the human resources person and she clearly indicated that the institution had taken the view not to allow nationals to work in their own countries at this lead position level. As I was leading the policy dialogue and managing the energy portfolio for a number of African countries, I asked her whether my manager would be informed that I was applying for a new job and at what stage. There was no doubt in my mind that if my manager were aware that I was applying for a new position before the end of the selection process, I would not get the position. I did not want anyone to be alerted before the time because it would derail my preparation process.

That day, I got home and informed Fatimata that the Almighty God was calling us to India. Why was I so sure? And why would the Lord call us so far away? She was not happy at the prospect of jumping again into the unknown, with her health issues, and going so far away from everything she had spent time painstakingly rebuilding after our return from Paris in 2001. Due to various conditions, I had determined long ago in my spirit that I was due to leave the Africa region department for another one within the organization and I was praying the Lord Jesus Christ to guide my steps. I was leading a team from an "ejection seat," but I was mentally prepared and ready to take off anytime. I had been discussing my next career move with my managers for the last two years. Obviously, these discussions were very cordial, with compliments about my strong performance and nice promises made, but I knew deep in my heart that a trap was slowly forming around me.

I repeatedly went to the Lord for direction, heeding the advice given by the Apostle James. "If any of you lacks wisdom, you should ask

God, who gives generously to all without finding fault, and it will be given to you. But when you ask, you must believe and not doubt, because the one who doubts is like a wave of the sea, blown and tossed by the wind" (James 1:5–6). I needed wisdom to maneuver in the troubled waters, and cried out for help[8] not to fall into the hands of my enemies. King David of Israel reaffirmed this principle of "not falling into the hands of one's enemies" when he was presented with three judgment options, as described in 2 Samuel 24:11–14:

> When David got up the next morning, the Lord had already spoken to Gad the prophet, David's seer: "Go, tell David, 'This is what the Lord says: I am offering you three forms of judgment. Pick one of them and I will carry it out against you.'" Gad went to David and told him, "Shall seven years of famine come upon your land? Or shall you flee for three months from your enemy with him in hot pursuit? Or shall there be three days of plague in your land? Now decide what I should tell the one who sent me." David said to Gad, "There is great distress to me. Let us fall into the hand of the Lord, for great is His mercy, but into the hand of man let me not fall!

Because the road ahead was unknown, we regularly set time aside as a family to pray about the move to India. Whenever the reluctance of moving out of our comfort zone would crop in and my wife and I would start arguing about whether this was the plan of God for us, I attempted to assuage her concerns by using a twisted version of Gamaliel's argument before the council. "For if their purpose or activity is of human origin, it will fail. But if it is from God, you

---

[8] Psalm 34:17: "The righteous cry out, and the LORD hears them; he delivers them from all their troubles."

will not be able to stop these men; you will only find yourselves fighting against God" (Acts 5:38–39). I would repeatedly tell her not to worry. If it was the Lord, everything would finally work out. If it was not, and any indication would come to confirm it, I would not resist and I would put the project to rest. It was very difficult for us to labor through that prayer, but I was determined to see the end of it as recommended by the Apostle Paul in Philippians 4:6–7: "Do not be anxious about anything, but in every situation, by prayer and petition, with thanksgiving, present your requests to God. And the peace of God, which transcends all understanding, will guard your hearts and your minds in Christ Jesus."

Whenever I would pray, mostly speaking in tongues, I would come out confident that our earthly journey was to include India. I would rejoice in the Holy Spirit about what was about to come and go to work peacefully. At that time, I was delegating more and more to my team members, making sure that I maintained the anchor of the program and provided overall strategic oversight. Fatimata, who shared the same professional background with me, started collecting information about the Indian power system, its status of development, the issues it faced, and the more she read and we discussed, the more it was clearer to us that the country was struggling to a certain extent as the African continent to address its basic infrastructure needs. My wife and I carefully reviewed my CV and she helped me rewrite it to address the job requirements. I waited until the last minute before I put in my application. We asked again for the Lord to guide the process and I forgot about it.

I went about my daily work, ensured that the delegation was as extensive as possible, and endeavored to stay afloat in the Holy Spirit as much as possible, obeying the injunction by the Apostle Paul in Ephesians 5:18, "Do not drink wine but be filled with the Holy Spirit and you will not accomplish the desires of the flesh." It was not the first time that I was going through such an experience of knowing that my end in a place was near and that soon I would take off again. I kept a distance with what was going on around me, with what people were telling me about the toughness of the portfolio I was handling, and surrendered everything into God's mighty hands as instructed in Proverbs 3:5–6: "Trust in the Lord with all your heart and lean not on your own understanding; in all your ways submit to Him and He will make your paths straight."

Whenever a colleague asked me how I was doing, the response was inevitably the same: "I am doing fine even though I am managing a portfolio of challenging projects in difficult country environments." I was assigned that job and as the centurion rightly said it in Matthew 8:9, "for I am under authority," and, fortunately, the one above the earth also knew very well the value of my service. The Lord Jesus Christ made me grasp long ago the importance of the work I have through the opening of my eyes on Colossians 3:23–24: "Whatever you do, work at it with all your heart, as working for the Lord, not for human masters, since you know that you will receive an inheritance from the Lord as a reward. It is the Lord Christ you are serving."

I went to meetings with the same passion, on business trips with the same feeling of isolation, but my focus on work was for Christ. Whenever I went to bed I slept in peace as experienced by the psalmist in Psalms 4:8: "In peace I will lie down and sleep, for you alone, Lord, make me dwell in safety."

Two months after the submission deadline, while I was again on a business trip to Cameroon, an African country that is in a time zone five hours ahead of the US, I read a "surprising" email informing me that I was selected for an interview. I read it twice to make sure that I was not dreaming. Yes, I was called for an interview, which meant that my application was favorably considered. I praised the Lord Jesus

Christ at my desk and continued my work on detangling some of the most intricate issues in the energy sector that were standing in the way of the development of a transformational project.

I called my beautiful wife in the US and informed her about the date and time of the interview. Just before the email came in, I was discussing with my manager the opportunity to make a presentation of the unit program at an international conference in France. I wanted to go to the conference, but my wife clearly advised me not to be distracted. As I was about to leave my unit, I focused my mind and thoughts on what lay ahead, drawing inspiration from the words of Apostle Paul in Philippians 3:13–14: "Brothers, I do not consider myself yet to have taken hold of it. But one thing I do: Forgetting what is behind and straining toward what is ahead, I press on toward the goal to win the prize for which God has called me heavenward in Christ Jesus." I managed to cancel my participation to the conference and went straight home to take advantage of the long weekend and finish my preparation for the interview. With my wife as coach, I spent many hours completing my data collection and structuring the information about the energy program in India. We used our family time on Saturday to pray specifically for the interview scheduled on Monday, and on Sunday, my wife and I had a special prayer time.

She battled for me, knowing that I had to go through the "eye of the needle" to reflect on the upcoming challenge, which could be akin to what the Lord said about the rich. "Again I tell you, it is easier for a camel to go through the eye of a needle than for a rich man to enter the kingdom of God" (Matthew 19:24). What else could I have done? I praised the Lord for the blessed opportunity.

On Monday morning, I was ready. Since it was also my first day back to work, I decided to go straight to the interview before heading to my department. I was early, and as I sat in the meeting room, I quickly got myself organized. I prayed in tongues, and as the Apostle Paul declared it in 1 Corinthians 14:4, I got edified. At the given time, the interview panel members started coming into the room, but the logistics were not yet in place for people who had to be connected from Canada, Afghanistan, the United Kingdom, and India.

Fifteen minutes later, the interview started. Various questions were asked about my teamwork, leadership skills, technical knowledge, and ability to handle sensitive policy dialogue. I thought the interview was easy when a question was asked about the portfolio and pipeline of the recruiting unit. Just before I left my house that morning, as I was preparing myself for the interview, I had told my wife that I felt the strong need to look at the unit's program because no one would expect me to lead without having an idea on the current portfolio and prospective program of the unit. I dug the information from the website, reviewed it, and printed a copy just in case. Little did I know that it was the Holy Spirit inspiring me for the final interview question. I pulled out my printout of the program and confirmed that I could work on all the activities listed, which was squarely true based on my background and the experience I had had so far. The interview adjourned on that question, and after the usual winding-down process, I left the room. Once outside, I praised the Lord that I did well and I committed the rest of the process to Him. I spoke to and thanked my wife for her stellar support, and confirmed that I delivered as per expectations. I went to my department and debriefed some of my colleagues about key events during my business trip and continued as if nothing was in the making.

My road had been rough since I left Togo, my country in 1994. I learned the hard way that more than allegiance was expected at every corner for some professionals. I also discovered that even if your supervisors were to stand in your face as if they were holding your entire life in their hands you should not be afraid because it is just an illusion. The Almighty God had taught me on this reality by using the following two portions of the Bible recorded in Matthew 10:28. "And do not be afraid of those who kill the body but cannot kill the soul; but rather be afraid of Him who can destroy both soul and body in hell [Gehenna]" and in John 19:11, where the Lord Jesus answered Ponce Pilate on the brink of His death: "You would have no power over me if it were not given to you from above."

When I received my annual evaluation toward the end of July 2007, I quickly realized that the write-up was full of subtle comments meant to be destructive. As I was going through these observations and thinking about how to address them, I went to work the next morning with my heart seeking a direction from the Lord. As I opened my emails, one drew my attention from the recruiting manager. He apologized for the delay in getting back to me and asked me to get ready for a second interview in a couple of days. The second interview was scheduled on a Saturday, but to my surprise, nobody showed up at the appointed time. I got another apology and we agreed to reconvene on another day. We managed to find a more convenient slot and we had the second interview.

It was now clear that I was ahead in the competition and I had to start working on the transition. It was such a sweet feeling to know that everything that had been engineered by the devil to make me fail hadn't worked out! I praised the Lord and thanked Him for the guidance and favor He gave me to go through these episodes without losing my faith in Him. I thought a lot about Fatimata, my dear wife, and praised the Lord for her sacrifice and sound advice. At that time, I was in the waiting for the final word. One day at the time, as recommended by the Lord in Matthew 6:34, "So do not worry or be anxious about tomorrow, for tomorrow will have worries and anxieties of its own. Sufficient for each day is its own trouble."

Finally, toward the middle of August 2007, although I was the winner recommended by the panel, my soon to-be-manager advised me that he had difficulties giving me the position because I did not have the required caliber and the breadth of experience, and that I should have "gray white hair" to stand as a lead in India. The thought flew through my mind that it did not matter whether my hair was gray, white, or of another color since I did not have enough hair anyway. My soon-to-be manager went on to say that he would have to build a case for me, "under-filling" the position for twelve months, and based on my performance, he would make the case for my promotion to GH (the highest technical level at that time). I had been there before, and it was obvious to me that after going through all the unfairness in the organization that another case was being set up. Yes, even by winning a competition, I was still viewed as "not so adequate." I was not surprised by the turn of events, but it was clear in my spirit that I had to leave my other position in the Africa region. I was in a situation where the fire behind me was bigger than the one that lay ahead of me. The Lord Jesus Christ had already given me sufficient indication that I was no longer needed. I thought I would get a decent treatment during the transition, but history was about to repeat itself, and since the Lord had already led me through the fire in so many occasions, I just needed to trust His infinite wisdom once more. Obviously, I was not happy, but I was ready because I knew that everything would work out for my good. "For we know that all things worked out for good for those who love God and have been called according to His purpose" (Romans 8:28).

For a position to be under-filled, a memo had to be prepared with the concurrence of the human resource department, the recruiting manager, and the "candidate" to lay out the expected results that would support the case for a promotion and describe the various steps of the process. Since there was no formal guideline, it was going to be tricky to safeguard my interests. I contacted the people I knew at various levels of the institution, but the Lord had not impressed upon the heart of anyone to raise a finger to help me. The future did not seem bright.

As usual with the Lord, to ensure that I did not use the excuse of not knowing His will, He put me just in a situation similar to the one the Israelites experienced when they were coming out of Egypt (Exodus 13–14) between the "Pharaoh behind, and the rocky mountains on both sides," and delineated a "narrow path" ahead. I did not have much choice. I had to go forward into the danger zone, and the Lord knew that I needed His grace and wisdom.

Drafting the memo was a tough negotiation process. It was clear from the first draft that the intention was to conclude the process without giving me what I had clearly won. In my subsequent discussions with several other people, I collected various pieces of the puzzle and toward the end of November 2007, just before Thanksgiving, the final draft was finalized with a start date of January 1, 2008. It took more than seven months to reach that end result. Since I was leaving my former unit and joining another one against the will of many people, I had to tread delicately to maintain a single point of accountability, come the assessment of my performance. To limit human influence, I restricted the information flows to my wife, besides the many pleas for deliverance to the Lord. What a funny situation! I had a source of mixed feelings about my upcoming transition, but even though I did not fully understand why I had to go through such a process, I trusted the Lord for leading me to my final destination. While many were expecting me to "compete" and "demonstrate" that I could succeed as a team leader in India, I also understood that I should position myself more as a "mentor" and raise the game to be a "servant leader" to my team. On that front, I believed I had learned valuable lessons during the past eleven years in the institution.

It is interesting to see how God has given to the world so many treasures in the Bible and that the Lord Jesus Christ has specifically taught His disciples key wise principles that the business world has adopted without following Him, let alone acknowledging Him. Among them, the concept of "wise partnership" and "servant leader" seemed particularly relevant for my move to India.

The idea of wise partnership is encapsulated in these words of the Lord recorded in Luke 6:39-49: "Can the blind lead the blind? Will they not both fall into the ditch?" The first time I came across that expression in the Bible, it struck a chord because of my severe myopia. When I don't have my thick glasses, it is very difficult for me to move around, and my wife doesn't want me to do anything delicate when I am in that situation. So to imagine someone else leading me in my condition, or even in a worse condition, is simply impossible. During my youth in Togo, or my subsequent trips in many African countries, I have come across blind men[9] being led by young boys, but these guides always had excellent vision because of their responsibilities. In the professional and political arenas, I have witnessed how leaders with strong convictions could lead others into the ditch because none of their followers were willing to challenge them to see whether they have better vision than their leaders. Thus confirming what the Lord said in Matthew 6:22–23: "The eye is the lamp of the body. If your eyes are good, your whole body will be full of light. But if your eyes are bad, your whole body will be full of darkness. If then the light within you is darkness, how great is that darkness!" Or, the prophet Isaiah's warning in Isaiah 5:20: "Woe to

---

[9] Usually as the result of river blindness. A disease caused by a parasitic worm (Onchocerca volvulus) that is transmitted by biting blackflies that breed in fast-flowing rivers. The adult worms can live for up to 15 years in infected persons, where they produce millions of worm embryos that invade the skin and other tissues, including the eyes, causing blindness

those who call evil good and good evil, who put darkness for light and light for darkness, who put bitter for sweet and sweet for bitter."

The principles of a servant leader were explained by the Lord to His disciples when He was about to leave the earth, and His disciples started arguing about who should be "the boss." As I was determined not to be led by any blind man, I was also resolved not to force my convictions down my team members' throats because I would "supposedly" be in charge. In describing the servant leader in Mark 10:35–45, the Lord told his disciples, "You know that those who are considered rulers over the Gentiles lord it over them, and their great ones exercise authority over them. Yet it shall not be so among you, but whoever desires to become great among you shall be your servant. And whoever of you desires to be first shall be slave of all. For even the Son of Man did not come to be served, but to serve, and to give His life a ransom for many." These words are powerful because they completely change the understanding one should have about leadership.

Yes, God was sending me to this new department with a specific vision, and He created the conditions for me to enter at the right level. The Lord was setting the scene and driving the circumstances to deepen my training.

CHAPTER SIX

LEAVING TOGO FOR ADDITIONAL TRAINING. IS IT GOD'S PLAN?

Kwawu

In 1990, between the end of my fourth year and the beginning of my last year in engineering school, several people asked me about my future plans. The normal course of action would have been to go back to Togo, but I had a strong feeling that I was still hungry for more. I started praying about the subject because I wanted God's direction.

A year earlier, another brother in Christ and a friend of mine, was in the same situation, and as we were praying together, God gave him the unequivocal answer that He wanted him to remain in his country after graduation. In my case, I was also willing to know the Lord's views and guidance, as I did not want to be out of synchronization with Him. About three months into the academic year, I had the dream of finding a solution to the power transmission issues in Africa, as I realized that without electricity it was difficult to reach a better economic situation. In class, we learned about new approaches to optimize the investment costs, but many African countries were still falling short of expanding electricity services to their populations. What could these countries do if they did not have electricity in big quantities? I understood that the Lord was directing me to pursue advanced studies in the electrical engineering field, with a focus on power transmission technologies. With that conviction, and with my academic performance and my young age at the time, it should have been possible to find some support to pursue my studies to the PhD level. I thought about changing the educational system, in particular going to an Anglophone environment such as in the US, but it was quite a long and lengthy process to complete and I did not have much time. I had to press on since I wanted to finish my studies as quickly as possible and dive deep into research.

I trimmed down my options to two possibilities, which were immediately relevant for a Togolese with my background: either to go to France (easier) or to go to Quebec in Canada (tougher). My parents, especially my mother, had asked me about my choice to help me build a strategy, which would have essentially consisted of identifying people in Togo to consult and seek their guidance. I could not answer them, since I did not have any specific direction from the Lord. I even came home for Christmas in 1990, to discuss my options with my parents' friends, but they advised me to do an MBA in the US after gaining at least two years of professional experience. But I was not interested in that option because I did not sense it was the direction of the Lord.

I kept praying about my projects and sent some applications, including one to the Ecole Polytechnique de Montreal. As I was praying, my conviction to go to Canada grew significantly because of their expertise in my field of interest. In May 1991, I got admitted. I received my letter of acceptance, which was valid for three semesters. Unfortunately, they did not extend any financial assistance, despite my duly motivated request. When I informed my parents that I got the key elements to go to Canada, the train had already left the station. My mother's contact in the Ministry of Higher Education told her that scholarships for Canada were already allocated and that

I had to wait for the next year cycle. She warned my mother that it would be very difficult to get a scholarship for Canada because the government tightly controlled the excellence scholarships given by Canada and only few, with the right political connections, could get them.

I was not deterred by the challenge and I prayed about it. I contacted several institutions, including the Canadian High Commission in Côte d'Ivoire, but their answer was always the same. I had to go back to Togo and get a scholarship from my government, and I was confident that the Lord would get me there. Is there anything impossible for Him? No matter how tough it turned out to be, I had the assurance that I would pursue my studies. In addition, since I received the direction after the administrative cycle in Togo, I knew I shouldn't worry. Didn't the Apostle Paul testify in Ephesians 3:20–21, "Now to Him who is able to do immeasurably more than all we ask or imagine, according to his power that is at work within us, to Him be glory in the church and in Christ Jesus throughout all generations, for ever and ever! Amen." At that time, our graduating class was actively preparing its study trip to Canada and everything was in place for it. We had great connections with the Canadian High Commission and they were extremely happy to sponsor our trip. I was especially counting on that two-week stay in Canada to meet my research director and explain my needs for financial assistance. However, the government of Côte d'Ivoire took the decision to privatize the National Electricity Utility and gave it to a French Company without any competition, while the Quebec Electricity Utility was also very interested and equally competent, having previously invested in increasing the awareness about a less costly North American technology of providing electricity. As a consequence, the Canadian government simply cancelled the trip. It was tough, but there was nothing that our graduating class could have done. Economic interests had clashed and we, African students, were one of the many casualties. We tried to explain to the Canadian Embassy that our cohort was diverse and they should allow the trip to go ahead, but there were ten Ivoirians in our group of twenty-five! And, as we were made to understand, the Canadian government was not ready to train African students, who would go back to work for another company. We were stunned! For my other schoolmates, it was just a trip that got cancelled, but for me, it was my whole strategy for success that was hit at its core!

The administration of our engineering college did not want our cohort to be the only one not going on a study tour, so they frantically worked with us to organize a trip to Tunisia and Morocco. At the end of the trip, I went back to Lomé, still expecting a divine intervention, but days went by quickly without any solution. I completed my paperwork and started my career as an electromechanical engineer at the Togolese Power Utility. While there, I sent a letter to the Ecole Polytechnique de Montreal to postpone my entrance, which was supposed to be in September 1991, to the next semester. Little did I know that the unfolding events[10] in the political sphere would significantly derail my plans. I was determined not to settle and I took drastic measures to be ready to take off whenever the Lord would open the door. I spent most of my days at work, focused on doing the best at every assignment and refusing to be compensated beyond my basic salary and benefits, as my eyes were on my next step, and on my departure to pursue my advanced studies. I was satisfied to return to my father's house and help with errands, the education of my younger siblings, and any other task I felt called to.

Shortly after joining my unit in the Togo electricity utility, the manager offered me positions that I could not take because they were

---

[10] I came back to Togo right after the National Conference of 1991 and everyone was excited to see the country embark on a bright path after the decades of dictatorship that plagued the country since 1967.

not consistent with my objectives. He also offered to compensate me for the extra work that I was doing, but I also declined because I did not want to entertain any false sense of comfort. I had to go, but I did not know when. I could have taken and saved the extra money that was offered to boost my meager[11] salary of about US$ 300–400 per month (120,000 FCFA). Since I did not have any immediate plans to get married, I did not feel the urge to earn that extra money.

After the three extensions that I could avail as per my acceptance letter, Ecole Polytechnique cancelled my admission in July 1992. If I had to go to Canada, I had to restart the process of admission. Since I could not go, and while I was waiting for the Lord's intervention, I continued to take care of my work at the company. The managing director and CEO of the utility company noticed the quality of my work and appointed me as head of the planning department for the entire company. The promotion was a great testimony of God's faithfulness, but it was still not what I wanted. I "reminded" God constantly about it through prayer and fasting as the Bible advised us in Philippians 4:6: "Not to be anxious about anything, but in everything, by prayer and petition, with thanksgiving, present your requests to God." I could see my dreams shrinking, but I decided not to give them up. There was no light in sight. Every time I sensed an opportunity, I talked about my dreams and hoped to influence Africa's destiny in the power transmission area. My father was the head of the National Electoral Commission, and through his contacts I met a Canadian expert who was convinced about my dreams and offered to help me manage through the administrative process. He wrote me a letter of recommendation to use for the renewal of my admission to the Ecole Polytechnique de Montreal (which I got in May 1994 for the September 1994 semester) and to seek financial

---

[11] For me, the pay was meager, but I was earning more than my mother, who had worked more than eighteen years in the public health system.

assistance from institutions outside of Togo. He also gave a word to my father that he was delighted to help such a dedicated young man and that my strategy sounded reasonable, which allayed my father's concerns that I was overly ambitious.

The people around me thought that dropping a promising career in the Togolese Electricity Utility was a huge mistake, but I needed to press on! I could have gone for the September 1994 semester, but because of some work assigned to me by the Lord, I decided to defer my admission to January 1995. Although I could not get a scholarship, I got in November 1994, through the Togolese Embassy in Canada, a letter that would allow me to pay the same fees as Canadian citizens. With that letter, there was a stark reduction in the tuition and financial requirements for a full year of study, one of the criteria for the visa application. After spending time in Togo and talking about my projects, I finally got all the elements in place to start preparing my trip to Canada. The last thing to secure was the visa, and for it, I had to go outside the country.

The visa process was shaky as it started off in Ghana and finished in Côte d'Ivoire. When I applied for the visa in Ghana, I had an altercation with an employee because he wanted to first ascertain the validity of my academic records before transferring my file to the right visa officer. It was a way for him to seek "additional compensation." In Luke 3:12–14, the Bible describes the concerns of "tax collectors who came to be baptized. "Teacher [John the Baptist], they asked, "What should we do?" "Don't collect any more than you are required to," he told them. Then some soldiers asked him, "And what should we do?" He replied, "Don't extort money and don't accuse people falsely—be content with your pay." Since I came in the Spirit and I had everything needed for my application, I did not want to suffer again at the hands of this corrupt employee! I knew nothing was missing in my file and I felt I had to retrieve my entire file immediately to resubmit my application in Côte d'Ivoire. This process would entail additional expenses, but I was ready for them. Canada was just a visa away! However, before returning my application file, the visa employee put a mark in my passport. The process, which was supposed to be straightforward, took another twist! I quickly came back to Togo, packed my belongings, and left for Côte d'Ivoire in the early days of December 1994. Would I get the visa this time? Nobody knew, but I did not have the choice. To carry out these trips, I took advantage of my annual leave and I was hoping to be able to come back to Togo before leaving to Canada for good. I applied for the visa as soon as I arrived. Although everything was in order, the process was delayed because of the mark in my passport. The Canadian High Commission in Côte d'Ivoire sent a request of information to their colleagues in Ghana to understand the reason for the mark but there was no response. I was going to the High Commission on a regular basis, but I was repeatedly told that no response had come in yet. I pleaded with the visa officer and reiterated the circumstances that led to my file withdrawal in Ghana. The officer confirmed that my file was complete and my background excellent and that there was no reason to deny me the visa, but he had to follow the administrative procedure. Finally, he called the officer in Ghana to get an answer to his query and the next time I saw him, he informed me that my visa application was approved and to come back in two days to get my Canadian visa. Finally, after three years, Canada was at sight.

I purchased my flight ticket and set my departure date to January 5, 1995. The visa process took so long that I could not go back to Togo, as originally anticipated, to say goodbye at my company as well as to my friends and leave on time for the beginning of classes at Polytechnique. In anticipation of a visa process being delayed, I prepared a letter asking for a one-year leave of absence to pursue further studies in case I could not come back.

My mind was now entirely focused on Canada, and since the Lord gave me the opportunity, I was not going to waste it; especially after all I had gone through. My moral and spiritual preparations were adequate, but I wasn't sure about my intellectual preparation, although I tried hard to maintain my scientific and technical knowledge while in Togo. I realized how hard it was to maintain sanity and sound ambition in the oppressing environment of the dictatorial regime that had extended its grip into every sphere of the country since 1967. My plan was very simple: I would go to Canada, and with the help and guidance of the Almighty God, my heavenly Father, I would discover a new way to transmit power and the African electricity problems would be solved for good. Once those were solved, economic growth could finally take place in all countries and prosperity could be extended to more people. With the abundant energy resources located in key countries, transmission of bulk electricity over long distances was the research field that needed the most attention, and Canada, especially Quebec, had some good experiences in that field.

I spent the rest of my stay in Côte d'Ivoire to thank the Lord for the breakthrough and visited very close friends. In the early days of January 1995, I finally took off and landed in Montreal as planned.

CHAPTER SEVEN

LIFE IN CANADA. DID I REALLY HEAR A CALLING FROM THE LORD?

Kwawu

A friend of mine came to pick me up at the airport of Montreal with a heavy coat! My clothing—specifically my two-piece suit and a woolen pullover—was too inadequate to brace such a rigorous winter. The moment my shoes touched the heavy snow, my toes froze and I started shivering. During the trip to my temporary residence—a student hall in the center of Montreal—I wondered if I had not picked the wrong time to land in Canada as snow was everywhere. It was dark and dirty on the streets, and so white and pristine on the trees and open fields. But since the Lord brought me to Montreal in the middle of the winter, it must have been the perfect time! My friend and I spent some time together to discuss my trip during those last moments in Africa, and he gave me some tips about living in Montreal. He then helped me find adequate winter boots, but even with those insulated shoes and several layers of socks, my feet could not get adjusted to the outside temperatures. I also realized that my skin would crack despite the heavy moisturizer I was using. However, I did not have time to concentrate on my physical adjustments, because classes started without delay.

My meeting with my director of research and the head of the electrical department was an interesting one. I explained to him that I did not have time to waste because I wanted to finish my PhD studies as quickly as possible and that I was planning to take four graduate courses during my first semester. He cautioned me that I was setting myself up for failure. The other reason for which I wanted to quickly finish was that I only had enough money to pay for a full year and I was counting on the Lord's grace to quickly establish a track record and apply for scholarship. I also asked my director if there were any teaching or research assistant positions available so I could earn some money. He told me of the few positions that were available, but they were competitive and no one would trust me as a newcomer. I was ready for the challenge.

I registered for the four graduate courses of relevance to my research. Most of the attendees were working professionals who were taking courses to advance their professional career. I had good rapports with my teachers, participated well in study groups, and really enjoyed my classes. I tried to build connections with the professionals who attended the classes by explaining to them why I was in Canada and what I was looking for. But I could not plant any lead to build on. I guessed I might have turned them down with these ambitious plans. Life was tougher than I could imagine, and the rigor of the winter was adding another layer of complexity. Fortunately, by the Lord's grace, I moved into a house with another friend of mine, who graduated from the same college in Côte d'Ivoire and came to Canada a year earlier on a scholarship from his government. We had a lot of fun together, discussing politics in Africa and solutions that Christians could bring to the table.

My first few days were disturbing. I had difficulties with old mathematical concepts, because I had forgotten many of the formulas and approaches, so I had to familiarize myself with tools I had learned in the past. Since the courses were at night, I had long days to study and prepare for them, and I quickly gained back my old skills and acquired new ones. Soon I was on top of the game in all of my classes. I started providing explanations to my fellow classmates who had academic difficulties, and to my great delight, I ended the semester with straight A's.

My director of research was impressed, and he offered me a research assistant position. My first task was to help him restructure and rewrite his book on overvoltages in high voltage networks for a lump sum of about Can$1,000 for an estimated six-month assignment. I was so proud to have secured such an assignment that the salary did not matter much, although by that time I started to realize how expensive it would cost to complete my studies after the recent policy changes at Polytechnique. Shortly after that, I also got an opportunity to work with Hydro-Quebec International on an interesting project linked to ferroresonance in distribution networks and its impact on design and planning processes. My academic results and these two assignments meant a lot to me. I viewed them as a testimony of God's faithfulness and confirmation that I was in His plan. I informed my parents that I was doing very well and on the right track to establish myself very soon as a distinguished scholar in the field of electrical engineering.

Things were rolling, but my financial situation was not improving. My budgeted expenses for the last part of my program exceeded my expected income, or what remained of the resources I had brought from my country. I had no assurance to get the money I lent to my friend to clear his huge phone bills, following the breakage of his relationship with his fiancée (who was in Côte d'Ivoire). In fact, as soon as we moved under the same roof, the problem with his fiancée started, and by the end of the third month, my friend has generated such huge bills on the house phone that the landlord started complaining overtly about the mess we had created in his house. Since he was my friend, I could not just leave him in the pit. How would I answer if the Lord ever asked me, "Where is your brother?" I hoped his emotional situation would improve quickly after we prayed about it, but it was not the case. My friend did not want to remain still. He would wake up in the middle of the night and called his ex-fiancée or a close friend of hers for long hours hoping to win her back. But nothing seemed to work. He was clearly disoriented, missing his bus stops, failing to turn in his assignments. I had to support him, alleviate his pains the best way I could, and hold his back while he was going through that difficult phase. Did not the Lord say in Luke 6:31, "And as you wish that others would do to you, do so to them"?

After going through this difficult period, I noticed that my friend was not taking any steps to pay me back. He got his monthly allowance and went about his life as if he did not have to do anything to reimburse his debt. I tried to talk about my upcoming financial problem and the fact that I needed money, but he did not even blink to offer any solution. Should I not have expected a different behavior? Were we not friends? Here I was, struggling for money. How would I recover? I was again counting on the Lord to find a solution. With my academic results in Polytechnique in hand, I did what I thought was appropriate. I talked to several Canadian institutions to get financial assistance. Everywhere I went, I saw posters offering financial assistance to students. There were plenty of opportunities and all you needed to do was to stretch your hand and grab them. But for every qualified applicant, there was another exclusive condition that I could not meet. You had to be Canadian citizen or permanent resident. I was repeatedly advised that I needed to change my nationality because a Togolese nationality was not good enough to open the Canadian success doors for me! But this verse of Jeremiah 13:23 came to mind: "Can an Ethiopian change his skin or a leopard its spots?" I entered the country as Togolese and I could not become a Canadian overnight unless I got married. Could I suddenly change my heart and forget about my fiancée that I loved so much and who was patiently waiting for me? There was no way I could even entertain a fake marriage. God brought me to Canada with a set of strings and I could not cut any of them without His authorization. Despite everything that I had done to prove myself, the only way to move forward was to change my nationality. If God was behind the project, I do not have to corrupt my dreams or myself. *Life is not fair,* I thought.

The Lord then orchestrated a plan that allowed me to explain my situation to the president of the Ecole Polytechnique de Montreal. After I paid the tuition for my summer semester and part of my fall semester, the finance department made a mistake and refunded me money. With that error, the school was losing Can$968.25 I was tempted to cash in the money and use it to partly pay for the rest of my fall semester tuition, which was coming due. If I returned the money, I would owe the school about Can$1,043.25 for the fall and winter semesters. Since I had done all the rounds, including pleading with my director of research to give me a monthly salary that would allow me to pay for my studies and take care of my living expenses, and found that there was no financial assistance available for me, I was back to praying and fasting to receive guidance from the Lord. I turned to the Apostle James's advice in James 1:5–7: "If any of you lacks wisdom, you should ask God, who gives generously to all without finding fault, and it will be given to you. But when you ask, you must believe and not doubt, because the one who doubts is like a wave of the sea, blown and tossed by the wind. That person should not expect to receive anything from the Lord."

As I was praying, the idea gushed into my mind that if I were to write to the president of Polytechnique and explained that I was returning money to Polytechnique instead of applying it to my fall semester tuition despite my financial difficulties, Polytechnique would hold onto its motto that "students were its first priority" and grant me some financial assistance. I attached my academic report and explained in the letter that I came from afar to study and planned to return to serve the African people. As expected, the letter drew his attention. I was contacted by the finance department of Polytechnique. I returned the money and also paid for the fall semester tuition with the remainder of the resources I had. Since I only had one course left in the fall semester to meet the course requirements, I intended to devote my winter semester to my master research thesis. I did not have enough resources to complete the winter semester, and the race started to find out how and why I came to this low point. I met with the international students' advisor and I broadly explained that my money was used to help a friend who could not repay me. He asked for a letter of recommendation from my director of research, which the latter did provide in such a graceful way that reinforced the conviction of the students' advisor that something wrong should have been at play. After several interactions between my director of research, the students' advisor, the finance department, and me, we came up with a budget of Can$4,000 and identified potential sources of financing among the departments at Polytechnique. Most people in Francophone Africa were suffering financially because of the Franc CFA devaluation, and there was no way I could go back to my parents and ask for any financial support. My brothers and sisters, back in my country, were entering or getting ready for college and it felt inappropriate to put an additional emotional and financial burden on my parents. I was in an awkward situation. Everyone could sense that I extended myself beyond my limits to help a friend. And there I was, sitting in front of people and asking for help.

I trusted the Lord Almighty before I embarked on this journey. I devoted all my energy and focus on coming to Polytechnique for a

PhD to the point where close friends and family members thought I was consumed by my ambition! I thought I was on the right track with the Lord's approval! Unfortunately, the winter semester has already started and a solution had to be found. I had earlier written to a CEO of a company in France, who had sponsored my participation in an international conference on large voltage networks in Paris in 1994, to explain my situation and ask for financial assistance for about Can$7,500 to complete my studies. But nothing came in as if heaven was closed! After gathering information from my director of research, the international student advisor asked me to prepare a letter providing the reasons for my situation. My cries for deliverance to the Lord were louder, but there still wasn't a response to clear the way.

What should I do? Should I resort to calling my parents and asking for their help again? Where would they find the resources? Should I take a small job somewhere in Montreal and violate the stipulations of my work permit, which had just been extended for one additional year? To complicate the matters, my friend became abusive and disrespectful, and since we could not pay the rent of the two rooms that we were occupying, the landlord asked us to share the same room. When would the Lord intervene? When would He shed some light over my situation? I was wrestling with these thoughts when I came to Polytechnique at 10:00 p.m. the night of January 23, 1996, to prepare the last piece of information required to finalize my application for emergency assistance.

As I sat down in front of the computer to draft the letter, I tried to see how I could present my situation without giving too many details about the ins and outs of my story. Was it not ridiculous that I sacrificed my dreams for a friend who did not even care? I realized that I could not describe any of the traumatic circumstances the Lord had led me through since I came to Canada. Doing so would have meant giving my friend and me up to sarcasm and ruining the Lord's reputation, as both of us claimed to be Christians. The only viable option was to surrender that dream of mine to the Lord! In defiance to the circumstances, I wrote in the letter that I decided to drop out of the program, and that I would come back next year. But in a soft voice, the Lord asked me what would happen if I could not come back. So I changed that sentence to read, "I would come back if conditions are warranted." At that moment, tears ran down my cheeks. I'd spent so much energy to keep my dreams alive to just drop them like that because the Lord had led me to an impasse, or rather; my obedience to the Lord had led me to an impasse! The whole episode lasted for about fifteen to twenty minutes, and suddenly I felt the peace of the Lord. The Lord Almighty whom I have trusted for so many years had put a stop on the project. What could I have done differently?

The next morning, I dropped the letter at the advisor's office and gave a copy to my director of research. About a week later, I received an unexpected phone call from France. It was from an employee of the company in France, the new CEO, who informed me that the retiring CEO gave instructions to give me half of the money (Can$3,750) I had asked for. He informed that he had taken so long to get back to me because he was busy preparing end-of-year activities and he'd almost forgotten about it. I could not believe it! Had this money come in a week or two ago, I would not have dropped out! I informed him that I was no longer a student. Nevertheless, I thanked him and asked for a confirmation, which he did the following day by fax. He offered apologies for not having anticipated the possible implications of his actions, but I reassured him that I would be fine, as I was mentally working on my way back to Togo. Since I did not know what the Lord was up to, I agreed with the CEO that I would later confirm if I still needed the money.[12]

---

[12] Toward the end of July 1996, I wrote the CEO a letter confirming that I no longer needed the money and released him from his promise to help.

CHAPTER EIGHT

FROM MONTREAL TO QUEBEC AND TO WASHINGTON, DC. THE LORD IS ALWAYS IN CONTROL!

Kwawu

The Lord continued to provide for my needs amazingly. I didn't know what the next phase would be, especially after dropping my ambitious plan. I did not have money and I had to live on a one-dollar meal per day. Around the same time, a conversation I had had previously about a stint to evaluate an energy efficiency program for an international organization based in Quebec City, a three-hour drive from Montreal, was revived. My friend who was supposed to undertake the assignment declined the offer because he'd gotten a better opportunity. The program director called me to find out about my availability. He insisted that I take the evaluation because I had been highly recommended to him. In the midst of my difficult situation, I saw this as a new door opened by the Lord. He is faithful and He promised not to forsake us.

A couple of days later, I was on my way to Quebec City. I was in deep emotional pain, but my mind wandered over the beautiful landscape as the bus drove down the road. Where would this new road lead me? As soon as I got to Quebec, I dived deep into my work.

It was my only way to cope, besides praying and reading the Bible. I was working from seven in the morning to late at night, regularly past midnight in the office, because I did not want my mind to think about anything or replay the various episodes of my Montreal adventure. I praised God that I did not lose my sanity, although I found myself many times thinking about how hurtful a betrayal of a friend could be. My mind kept going back to Psalm 41:9 where, in anticipation of the betrayal of Jesus, the psalmist said, "Even my close friend, whom I trusted, he who shared my bread, has lifted up his heel against me." Yes, my final days with my friend in Montreal were painful, and I literally had to flee from his presence because of his verbal abuse and ill manners. I left, in secret, without leaving any point of contact. As I was leaving, the Holy Spirit comforted me with these words in 2 Corinthians 4:16–18: "Therefore we do not lose heart. Though outwardly we are wasting away, yet inwardly we are being renewed day by day. For our light and momentary troubles are achieving for us an eternal glory that far outweighs them all. So we fix our eyes not on what is seen, but on what is unseen, since what is seen is temporary, but what is unseen is eternal."

With the money I earned, I started planning my return to Africa. As per the letter my parents forwarded me, the Togolese Electricity Utility denied my request for a leave of absence for the duration of my studies and conveyed that I was no longer an employee. I could buy a return ticket, but I needed a little more to start something on my own. While in Quebec City, I again contacted a professional at the World Bank who I had met in Togo just before I left, probably in September 1994, and he told me that he would need someone to conduct a planning study on the electrical energy balance in the West African region. I knew that region very well, as I used to study the impact of the looming electricity supply-demand imbalance on the Togo–Benin economies and how, without rigorous planning and a financing plan, these economies would be badly hurt by the cyclical drought that affected the area. He asked his assistant to send me the recruitment forms, which I filled quickly and sent them to the World Bank human resources department. A couple of weeks later, I was offered a three-month assignment that was to start on March 11, 1996. When I went to the American Embassy in Quebec City for the visa and showed them the letter of employment from the World Bank, the visa officer diligently processed my file, and in one hour, I got my visa to the US. When I compared the struggle to get the Canadian visa to the ease with which God gave me the American visa, I could not help thinking that the Lord acted in mysterious ways! On one side, it was a rollercoaster, but on the other side, the matter sailed through quickly like a letter at the post office.

From the time I left Montreal to my arrival in Washington, DC, on March 9, 1996, there was no gap in my schedule, as the Lord at each step faithfully led me to a secure place. My thoughts were still on the return to Togo, which I had planned to do after the completion of my assignment in Washington, DC. While at the World Bank, I maintained the same routine of coming to work very early, with a one-hour break around three to go for a walk and talk with the Lord, and leaving late, usually after eight. I quickly finished my first assignment, started a new one and finished it also, and by the end of the initial three-month period, I was done with my two assignments and had plenty of free time. The team leader I was working with asked me about my future plans. I told him that I was done with pursuing my studies at the PhD level and I was planning to go back to my country soon after my assignment. He told me he needed someone to help with project management and procurement and if I was interested.

Thanks to the intranet, I had learned a lot about the World Bank from the inside and found out that the salary I was so happy about was indeed lower than what I could have earned, were the rules applied. So, I told my team leader that I should be treated fairly. I was not asking for a particular favor but just to be treated fairly! I was also later told that since I joined as a project assistant, there was no way my situation would change, especially with my salary level. Had the Lord led me again into another trail of injustice? I kept asking the Lord if there was nothing else He could have done for me. I was coming out of a difficult situation and I was neither mentally prepared nor ready to sustain another "painful episode." I kept on complaining in my mind as if He was not in control of every situation, as if He had not promised and declared that we would not be tempted beyond our strength! What a pretentious stance on my side! I guess, I got "on His nerves," because one day, as I was repeating the same tirade, I heard a clear voice say, "SHUT YOUR BIG MOUTH! YOU DO NOT UNDERSTAND THE WAYS OF THE LORD!" Frightened that I had crossed a line, I bowed in my spirit and closed my spiritual "mouth." After that incident, I thought of the terms of the dialogue God had with Job when he reached the end of his strength and faith in the Almighty God. In Job 38:1–7, it states, "Then the Lord spoke to Job out of the storm. He said: 'Who is this that obscures my plans with words without knowledge? Brace yourself like a man; I will question you, and you shall answer me.'" I did not have anything for my defense. God has faithfully provided anything and everything I've needed!

I got a five-month contract extension, and another fourth-month extension, bringing the total work duration to one year, when factoring in the initial contract of three months. In 1997, at the one-year renewal period, I got a salary increase of four percent, bringing it to about $35,000 per year. I did not know what tomorrow would be career-wise. No one in the office wanted to commit, although I was performing above a satisfactory level. But I was no longer in the mood of fighting with God. I spent my time working as hard as before and not changing any bit in my daily routine. I was under the oversight of the Almighty God! He led me into my situation and He was still leading me. I thought the situation would linger for a while, but as the Lord Almighty promised, He was always on time!

After a certain time, a new manager came onboard in August 1998, and he decided to correct the discrepancies between my workload and my compensation package. A year later, he offered me a permanent job after a competitive process. While going through that process, I was also selected to be a senior power engineer in an investment bank in Paris and I was to spend two years in France starting from September 1999. In a matter of three years, since I joined the bank as a project assistant, the Lord had upheld my rights and opened new doors for me. When I came back from Paris two years later I had to start afresh, but this time with a better entry point as a power engineer, a grade below the position I had in Paris. I got promoted to senior power engineer in 2003 after another manager thought I was unfairly treated given my strong performance. Since my return, I had been handling tough assignments. Irrespective of the results, I tried to abide by the instructions given in 1 Corinthians 10:31: "So whether you eat or drink or whatever you do, do it all for the glory of God." From my Christian perspective, the Lord, who sees everything, knows exactly the value of your work and the truthfulness of your worship! Didn't the Lord say to His disciples in Luke 17:10, "So you also, when you have done everything you were told to do, should say, 'We are unworthy servants; we have only done our duty'"?

When I gave my life to the Lord Jesus Christ in 1986, I was puzzled about the value of secular work. I wanted to enter into the full-time pastoral ministry but the Lord reiterated that He was the one who assigned responsibilities. Yes, He has assigned specific ministries described in Ephesians 4:11 meant for the edification of the Body of Christ, of which I am a full and integral member, but He carries His work in the world through the members of the Body as He sees fit. Thus, as long as I carry a specific assignment that He has instructed me to do, at His own time and according to His Sovereign will, I should rejoice that I have obeyed the Lord. I just needed to do whatever He assigned me to, irrespective of any other considerations I might view as valid. Being a servant requires the discipline of obedience, and practicing servant hood always positions you in God's eye as a leader. Didn't the Lord Jesus Christ tell His disciples in Matthew 22:26–27: "But you are not to be like that. Instead, the greatest among you should be like the youngest, and the one who rules like the one who serves. For who is greater, the one who is at the table or the one who serves? Is it not the one who is at the table? But I am among you as one who serves." While I thought this would apply primarily in the church, my understanding was broadened by the words of the Apostle Paul to Ephesians: "Slaves, obey your earthly masters with respect and fear, and with sincerity of heart, just as you would obey Christ. Obey them not only to win their favor when their eye is on you, but as slaves of Christ, doing the will of God from your heart. Serve wholeheartedly, as if you were serving the Lord, not people, because you know that the Lord will reward each one for whatever good they do, whether they are slave or free" (Ephesians 6:5–8). So whether I am a bondservant or slave, it should not matter.

All I needed was to be sure that God was actually the one leading me into "slavery" for His own glory. Here I was, having left Africa with the highest expectations of scientific discovery and deliverance from poverty but now being led by the Lord through "tortuous" ways and painful experiences to be obedient to His ways! Accepting God's guidance and obeying His will always require faith, and that it is why the Lord Jesus Christ gave that stern warning in Matthew 7:21–23: "Not everyone who says to me, 'Lord, Lord,' will enter the kingdom of heaven, but only the one who does the will of my Father who is in heaven. Many will say to me on that day, 'Lord, Lord, did we not prophesy in your name and in your name drive out demons and in your name perform many miracles?' Then I will tell them plainly, 'I never knew you. Away from me, you evildoers'!"[13] Did He not say in Mark 10:45: "For even the Son of Man did not come to be served, but to serve, and to give his life as a ransom for many"?

In my search for freedom and space to live according to God's calling, I was about to be thrown again into an adventure, but this time I knew a lot more and I understood a little better what could be at play. Without any pressure, I was about to enter a new episode of my life and this time, with my family, since there was no way for me to go to India alone. The Lord had already confirmed that it was time to move out of Washington, DC.

[13] In KJV version, the expression "you evildoers" is replaced by "you who practice lawlessness!"

CHAPTER NINE

GETTING READY FOR THE MOVE: FIRST IMPRESSIONS OF INDIA

Fatimata and Kwawu

Fatimata: Will we or will we not go?

Given the controversy about our move to India, my husband and I agreed that we would pray and let the Lord Jesus Christ bring us to the same understanding of His will. Although not very enthusiastic, I tried to be as helpful as I could to my husband by letting myself be conducted by the Holy Spirit during his preparation, especially because he was also moving into unknown territories. The research on India threw out several interesting documents, and because India was on the world's radar screen, my husband was able to learn from different sources. He had successful interviews, and despite the obstacles, we patiently waited for the final outcome. It took about three months between winning the competition and the decision to award the position. It was finally in late November 2007, seven months after the start of the process, that an agreement was reached on the date of my husband's transfer from his old unit. However, given the above difficulties and the fact that we were moving to a country with anticipated culture differences, our move to Delhi was set loosely in the summer 2008 to allow a gradual adjustment to his new posting.

Fatimata: *What would my husband discover during his first visit to India?*

As the date of his departure was getting closer, two sets of feeling were clashing: for him, the excitement was growing, and for me the feeling was mixed since I could not really adjust to the idea of leaving behind all my familiar surroundings, especially after the almost seven years after our return from Paris in 2001. And we also had to prepare our children for the move. When my husband left, I tried to talk to my ten-year-old son and my eight-year-old daughter about a possible move out of the US. The news was a shock, as they did not want to move away from their friends and aunties. The children begged me not to take them out of the country for three years, asking instead for a short vacation. I was really troubled and could only find peace in prayer. The more I prayed, the more peace grew in my heart about the idea. "Do not be anxious about anything, but in everything, by prayer and petition, with thanksgiving, present your requests to God. And the peace of God, which transcends all understanding, will guard your hearts and your minds in Christ Jesus" (Philippians 4:6–7). My husband spent ten days in India and we could not wait for his return. What went through his mind from the day he took off from Washington, DC, on December 10, 2007?

Kwawu: *What would this unknown developing country reveal?*

I had been to different places in the world, but this was my first trip to South Asia. I needed first to explore the land. My itinerary required that I transit through London to go to India. The flight segment between Washington and London was a simple one; all I did was sleep. When I was boarding the plane in London, the impression of going to a different continent suddenly became big and strong. As I was walking to the plane, I was surrounded by many similar faces, some with turbans, who were looking at me, probably wondering where I was going and what for. On the plane, I spent time reviewing the road traveled and figuring out what could be the possible outcomes of my trip.

After another eight hours, I landed in the middle of the night in New Delhi. The airport looked so crowded, and people were rushing to the immigration counters. I looked around, saw the counter for diplomats and officials, and resolutely walked there. I felt people's intense curiosity about me, but I chose to attribute it to the black hat and black coat that I was wearing. I cleared immigration and customs, and the office driver joyfully welcomed me. We started a conversation about me, my family, and life in India. He was very friendly, but I had to really focus to understand him. I fervently hoped that our trip to India would not be constrained by the language barrier. Fortunately, I was able to get most of the substance of his tips. He even suggested that I spend five years in India and visit as many different places to get a good understanding of the country. As we were driving to my hotel, I got a little sense of the "orderly chaos" of the place. Overloaded trucks with goods stacked beyond the permissible height were speeding past equally overloaded cars with excess number of passengers. I had the impression that everyone everywhere was honking and looking to find their way on somehow narrower roads than I was used to in the US. As I observed the dusty roads, the unfinished buildings, and the road construction sites, my mental adjustment process kicked in. The giant called India was in transition, but it looked very much like a conglomeration of the various African cities I have cruised through before. The place suddenly looked so familiar to me. With the roundabouts, the way people drove in the streets with limited observance of traffic rules, the mixture of old and not-so-old buildings, and the greenery, the place evoked a blend of Nairobi, London, and Accra. This was perhaps a residual effect of the British colonization.

During my ten-day stay, I went on several short city visits to find reasons and trinkets to convince my dear wife that India was indeed the next step of our earthly journey. I was clearly in a developing country, with the blend of beautiful and not so beautiful, of clean and not so clean, and of rich and not so rich. My convictions about the language barrier grew stronger when I had my first meetings with my Indian colleagues. Whenever the topic became interesting, people would commute into Hindi. I had to ask to repeat in English to get a sense of the passionate statements made. I thought about how to overcome this language barrier that created isolation. Nevertheless, I managed to glean out the information I was looking for, except for perhaps the most important information.

The final issue to address was to find a genuine evangelical church. With all the idols (Acts 17:16-34) on almost every street corner, the altars to the numerous deities, I quickly realized that the idea of a unique Almighty God was absent. How can they survive with so many gods? The shapes of these gods were very strange to me: many of them have mere or enhanced human bodies, and animal heads (monkey, elephant, etc.) and some have animal bodies and human heads. How would we handle this spiritual shock? Didn't the Lord, God Almighty, command in Deuteronomy 5:8–9 that "You shall not make for yourself an image in the form of anything in heaven above or on the earth beneath or in the waters below. You shall not bow down to them or worship them; for I, the Lord your God, am a jealous God." How would my wife and kids react to these images? This stood in stark contrast with what I had seen in Africa, Europe, and America. I tried to make sense of the new religious framework, which evoked a blend of animism and polytheism, but I was curious to find out how this would impact values and behaviors. Being African, I have seen how animism, presented as a cornerstone of our ancestral values and pride, has destroyed the society and brought peoples and nations under a malignant spell, crippling individuals into fear and slavery. When was this spiritual state of affairs established? I just thought that the spiritual atmosphere in the country was so far away from our reality. This increased my desire to find common grounds or anchors. I surveyed the hotel directory, searched the Internet, and talked to many of the taxi drivers to find Christian libraries. Finally, one of the attendants at the hotel concierge desk suggested a small bookstore not too far from my hotel. The bookstore had several of the traditional Christian literature, CDs, and DVDs I could find in the US. I asked the librarian about Indian Christian artists and he suggested a couple of articles, which I bought. In the store, I met with some Christians and our exchanges reassured me that we could find a good place to worship the Lord. I knew deep in my heart that the Lord was leading us and concluded that we would be fine in India.

As a result of all my outings and shopping tours, I came back home with a black Sherwani (Indian garb) embroidered with gold patterns, a set of Christian Video CDs and CDs, Indian women suits for my daughter and wife, and one *kurta* pajama for my son. I gave them their gifts that cost me a lot, proudly put on my Sherwani, and was hoping for a good time of laughter!

Fatimata: *What kind of gifts are these?*

My husband was really excited to show us the numerous presents he brought from his exploration. He gave me a set of traditional clothes, but when I saw the two-piece ensemble, I just knew the top would not fit and the pants were two big. My husband insisted that it was pure silk, making me feel the quality of the embroidery to convince me that he'd bought a quality item. He was told in India that it was a one-size-fit-all suit and that it should fit. But it was disappointing: the clothes did not fit, and I did not find them beautiful. I then asked him how he managed to get those articles, and he explained that he'd relied on trusted advice and was persuaded that everything would be fine.

Since he did not get the expected emotions from me, he was waiting for the kids' reaction. He went to the kids' rooms and asked them about their outfits. Our daughter was happy to wear her suit, although she was already on the brink of outgrowing it, and our son looked at his *kurta* pajama and thought it was a girly dress. My husband tried to convince him that it was worn on wedding days or for big ceremonies, but my son reiterated that he could not imagine wearing that suit outside the house. My husband's disappointment showed on his face. We all laughed about his failed attempt and we then moved to the other set of presents, the Christian VCDs. Since my husband primarily wanted Indian artists, he could only get VCDs. The VCDs he had selected had interesting testimonies and Christian songs and we quickly zapped through them with our children. We could see the influence of American culture in some of the songs; however, the beat, the way of speaking, and the dances were inviting. On that front, both my husband and I were satisfied. He finished unpacking his luggage, and he let us know that he would be more careful next time during his gift selections.

After my husband's first experience, I was not that impressed by India. I knew I needed to learn more about the country before our family moved there. I had many questions: How was he treated? What places did he visit? Were the positive testimonies I received about places, behaviors, attributes, and peculiarities a true reflection of the reality, or were they tainted by my husband's optimism?

On adjusting to New Delhi, he convinced us that he was looking forward to a nice familial experience as he described some of the traits of the cities. He also added that it was particularly striking to see people with arms or legs missing, thin-haired children with deep eye sockets and runny noses. Although he had been in touch with a certain level of poverty before, even in capital cities in Africa, he had to admit that it was by far greater than he expected. I wondered if we could walk through this experience unscathed. I did not mention any of this to the kids since I knew how traumatized they were by human misery when they'd gone on vacation in Africa. If this was more than what they have already seen, I wondered how it could affect them. I needed wisdom to speak to them and I got back to my trusted source: the word of God. As said in James 1:5–8: "If any of you lacks wisdom, he should ask God, who gives generously to all without finding fault, and it will be given to him. But when he asks, he must believe and not doubt, because he who doubts is like a wave of the sea, blown and tossed by the wind. That man should not think he will receive anything from the Lord; he is a double-minded man, unstable in all he does."

We had several discussions about how we could help and concluded that we would embark on this Indian experience with an open mind and count on the Lord's guidance. We spent the Christmas and New Year break visiting friends and my husband shared some of his experiences. I was sometimes excited, sometimes concerned about my health, and sometimes sad about leaving my sisters and friends behind. Of course, many of my questions did not receive a complete answer from my husband, and he promised that he would observe more during his next business trip, and we had to agree on the type of information he needed to collect.

Fatimata: *Second Visit to New Delhi: Would He Properly Finish His Exploration?*

For the preparation of the second trip, my husband and I reviewed the questions for which I needed information. I wanted him to be thorough in his observations. He was already settled on the move but

I needed more. He was so upbeat that I wondered if we were on the same wavelength. I decided to pray more with our children about our concerns for our next move such as my health, finding a good school for the kids and their adjustment to the new environment, a suitable place to live, and a good community. I could not help but think about my health. I would often go through flashbacks, and unpleasant memories regarding my health would surface. I wondered how my body would react, and I asked myself over and over if this trip was really something I wanted to do. Was it the fear of the unknown that was making me so uncomfortable or was it something else? Did God not say in Isaiah 43:2–3: "When you pass through the waters, I will be with you, and through the rivers, they will not overwhelm you. When you walk through the fire, you will not be burned or scorched, nor will the flame kindle upon you"? But if He wasn't leading us, how would I survive? If it were Him, He would take us through this journey safely.

Praying got so difficult. As described by the Apostle Paul in Romans 8:26, too often the Holy Spirit came to my aid and bore me up in my weakness. The Spirit Himself pleaded on my behalf with unspeakable yearnings and groaning too deep for utterance. I would often pray in tongues as the Bible declared in 1 Corinthians 14:4 that "He who speaks in a tongue edifies and improves himself." I really wanted the Lord to lighten up my burden. I was overwhelmed by all the numerous subjects of concerns and tasks to complete before our move that my only refuge was to trust the Lord. My husband finally took off for his second ten-day trip in mid-January 2008.

Kwawu: Would this second exploratory business trip truly expand our knowledge?

I thought one trip would be enough to erase all my wife's doubts, but it was not the case. Because of the many questions I could not answer at the end of my first trip, I carefully prepared my second visit, writing down all the questions for which I needed to collect information before I took off. The sixteen-hour trip went by quickly. My mind was focused on my assignment, and as soon as I landed, I paid close attention to details and started looking around for a place to live. With my wife's health situation, we needed to do a detailed and careful screening to find a decent place, in a not-so-polluted neighborhood, and close to medical facilities where we could go to in case of emergency.

I was told that the housing market was booming and that rental prices had skyrocketed, but with the high rental budget, about US$7,000 equivalent per month, I was confident that we could find a nice apartment that was properly positioned. As I was discovering new facets of India, the transition between Delhi and other cities, I realized that India was far too complex to decipher. You have to understand the body and head languages, which is quite an art. To be more convincing next time with my wife, I needed precise answers, so I decided to repeat my questions to my interlocutors until I obtained a decent response. I had to double or even triple-check to ensure the accuracy of the information. It helped sometimes, and sometimes it didn't. Some realtors contacted me and through them I visited some houses and a few apartments. I finally settled on the idea that a ground floor and basement apartment in a gated community would meet our family needs. The rationale was very simple: the ground floor would be our living space and the basement the children's dedicated play area. Since we were in the middle of January, I was told that the rental market was not active, and as the move was anticipated in the summer 2008, there was no need to rush. The few properties I had visited were not very new and one could see that they had not been properly maintained. By talking to several expatriate colleagues, I also got the sense that we had to lower our expectations, and we had to be prepared to spend time and financial resources to upgrade whatever place we would find to our liking. The stories about failed appliances due to voltage fluctuations, deficient plumbing systems as a result of inadequate maintenance, and inordinate long repair times were rather disturbing. There were great reminders that a high rental budget was meaningless in a market with shortages of good properties. I could not contemplate spending so much time supervising repairs at our future place.

As usual, the business side of my trip was excellent. I had several interesting meetings with my colleagues and the clients. I reported the outcome of my trip to my wife and started to actively work on the move.

Fatimata: *Did we really understand God's plan for us?*

My husband did not provide too many details about the properties he visited. He did not want to tone down my high expectations about where we would land, but he categorically ruled out living in a house. According to him, a house would require extensive maintenance and he did not want to spend time chasing handymen. Although I knew that India was a developing country, I was hoping that we would find a suitable and comfortable place, which we could temporarily call home.

My husband was no longer confident about finding a decent place. I could sense his assurance diminishing, which was not the case after his first exploratory trip. I was again troubled and started doubting our move. We prayed again about it and committed every step into the Lord's hands, as recommended by King David in Psalm 37:5: "Commit your way to the Lord; trust also in Him and He will bring it to pass." It was becoming even harder to tell our kids that they would have to leave their environment for an unknown place in India. We discussed and prayed as a family, allowing everyone to share their feelings about the summer move. The feelings were not very great. But every time I talked to my family in Burkina Faso and my mother would enquire about our upcoming move, I would put on an air of positivity. As my husband was so convinced about Delhi being part of the earthly journey, I also needed to be ready for the move.

Professionally, I could see how the pieces fit together for my husband but on my side, I needed to take it by faith. I was still struggling to find the right balance. I was the most concerned, as I had to deal with my health issues and the well being of my children, which was not easy. On top of all that, I had to leave again my professional life behind and start over after several years of work.

CHAPTER TEN

JOINT VISIT TO INDIA: WILL FATIMATA BE CONVINCED?

Fatimata

My husband and I agreed that I should go to India with him in February 2008 and see the country for myself. The delicate part was to be prepared to handle my body's reactions to the high pollution levels and any asthma attack. In his previous trips, my husband had taken several pictures from his hotel room where I could see large amounts of smog. We took extra care to have all my medicines in large enough quantities, and prepare for the worse without any immediate help in sight. Whenever I would raise any doubt or question the relocation to India, my husband's response was invariably that "we have to obey the Lord, and if He is taking us somewhere, it is for a purpose." Before the discussion went off-track, he would tell me not to worry, because if we weren't convinced that India was in the Lord's plan for us then he wouldn't take the job.

Despite all the preparation, I was not relieved and fear seemed to grip my heart. How could I experience such strong feelings of fear when the Lord in Matthew 6:27 encouraged us to be free of worry? "And who of you by worrying and being anxious can add one unit of measure to his stature or to the span of his life." Another complicating factor for the February 2008 trip was to find alternative arrangements for our two children. They needed a transportation arrangement to go to school and a place to live while we were gone. My sisters offered to be the guardians of their nephew and niece, so all we had to do was to find a good transportation arrangement. After much thinking, we selected a taxi driver who often took my husband to the airport for his professional trips. We agreed on the price and on a schedule that would allow the kids to be at school on time in the morning and be brought home after their after-school activities. We even gave the driver extra money to motivate him and ensure that he would be on time and the routine would be flawless.

I talked to several of my Indian colleagues, our Indian neighbors, and the Indian shopkeeper around the block to build my knowledge of the host country. Since I was traveling with my husband, I got a business visa to India for a full year and multiple entries. This business visa was really a blessing (as we would later discover) and allowed me to work in India. We completed our preparations, both at work and at home, and took off. We had a packed agenda because I planned to meet several people to triangulate the information my husband had collected. I wanted to ensure that we had considered every possible scenario. For my husband, it was his third trip, but it was my first visit, and my husband was clearly more comfortable. However, he was nervous about how I would like the country where we would be living for the next three years.

As soon as the flight took off from Washington, my husband fell asleep. I tried to wake him up to keep me company but he wouldn't budge. That first leg from Washington, DC, to London was too long. I could not sleep for a second and I kept thinking about our kids, their transportation arrangements, and how my health would be affected by the pollution levels. By the time we reached London, I was exhausted. Our transit time in London was only about two to three hours and we soon had to get on the flight to New Delhi, India.

What a shock when we arrived at the airport gate for Delhi! I felt as if everyone was staring at me! I thought our fellow Indian passengers were rude. They were staring at us without refrain. My husband had told me about his previous experience, but I was not prepared for being stared at. What a difference between the attitude of people in the US and the attitude of Indian people! My whole impression of India started to tilt, and although my husband tried his best to distract me, the bad impression did not falter. Once the plane took off, I was able to sleep for small periods at a time.

We landed in New Delhi around 1:45 a.m. From the plane windows, the city was dark, the vision blurred, and the lighting not very impressive. When we stepped out of the plane, people were pushing and rushing to reach the immigration counters. As we had a special status, we went to the official counter. Again, so many people were staring at me, probably curious to know where we were coming from. I was later told that my braided hair might have contributed to the attraction of focus. The airport was undergoing renovation, and it did not look impressive. I started complaining about breathing problems, and I wasn't sure if it was attributed to the long trip or the dust in the airport. Sensing a storm, my husband quickly said that the air was fine as he was breathing normally. I was not. By the time we collected our luggage and reached the outside gate of the airport, it was getting close to 3:00 a.m. I was already suffocating and used my rescue medicine several times in less than fifteen minutes.

Would my first visit be a flop? We took a cab, not very shiny, and the taxi driver did not want to put the air conditioner on because it was relatively cold outside. It was February, but the outside air was unbearable and unsustainable. My husband then firmly asked the driver to close the windows and put the air conditioner on. We were heading to the Imperial Hotel, one the best hotels in town and highly recommended. During the trip to the hotel, I wondered if the gloomy landscape was close to the India I portrayed in my mind. In a course of twenty-four hours, the disillusion was so stark that my husband was constantly referring to the hotel as a safe haven. He was hoping that the stay at the Imperial Hotel would help me overcome my disastrous feeling.

When we checked in at the hotel forty-five minutes later, the first thing I rushed to do was to find out about our children. I wanted to know if the taxi driver picked them up as per our agreement. My husband was against the idea and advised me to take some rest but I could not. I wanted to know about the children's first day of school without both of us. I called one of my sisters around 4:40 a.m., which was about six p.m. in Washington the previous day, and she indicated that the driver did not show up and my other sister went to pick them up by metro bus. I could not get through to her!

We immediately called the driver. He gave us the excuse that his car had broken down and he could not show up at the kids' after-school program. This was the last thing I needed! I almost collapsed! To know that our children were not picked up from school made my heart pound! The panic escalated, and in a matter of seconds, I regretted having come to India. My husband took the phone and conveyed his strong disappointment to the driver.

What could we do in the middle of the night from across most of Asia and an ocean? Nothing . . . except to praise the Lord Jesus Christ and ask for His help (Isaiah 43:2; 1 Corinthians 10:13). I spent the rest of the night until dawn calling Washington to find out if our children had made it home safely. When I finally got the children, they were happy to have taken the metro bus with my sister and described how they'd spent their day. By that time, it was already six in the morning. We had to rest and prepare for the day. For my husband, it was his first day of work, and for me, it was my first day in India.

All plans had been made for my first trip to be a nice one. Although my husband told me that it was one of the best hotels in the region, I was not impressed. The hotel did not have all the amenities for me to feel comfortable and I didn't think the breakfast was great either. To keep things in perspective, I reminded myself that we were in India as a couple to collect whatever useful information we could for the relocation process.

At ten a.m., I stepped outside the hotel, and my rental car was surrounded by a group of the poorest of the beggars I had ever encountered, and that was a shock to me. Even though I was born and raised in Africa, it was a completely new and hard experience for me to see so many poor people. I learned later on that beggars in the streets or at crossroads were actually controlled by gangs that was why they were so fearless to conduct such an illegal activity, even in front of policemen. By the time the driver drove through the city to my destination, I was emotionally drained. The traffic was really bad! I constantly thought the taxi was going to get in an accident. There were so many cars and two- or three-wheelers. Wow, driving was violent and erratic in Delhi! And with the cows in the street, it was really mind blowing! My husband had previously described Delhi's traffic, but I could not have expected it to be so bad. From my first meeting to the second, the car got caught in a traffic jam, and I could not reach my meeting place in the afternoon.

When my husband and I met in the evening at the hotel, the damage was already done. I was extenuated and disappointed about not having completed my program. In addition, I had headaches, body aches and I was shivering. In the middle of the night, my condition worsened and we had to make an emergency call for the hotel doctor. He was quick to come and after checking my vital signs, and he concluded that I might have an infection. Since he could not carry any exams, he did not give any name for my disease but advised that antibiotics would help. He gave me some antibiotics and another tablet for the fever. From what I recall, the medication did not have a proper label, but I just swallowed the pills without questioning. All I wanted was to get better and go back to the US to see my precious kids. Until today, I do not know the name of the medications but they did work. I spent most of my time in the hotel, lying in bed and recovering from the sickness. For the following three to four days, I used my nebulizer several times and tried to think positively about the move.

I now knew in my flesh what it would be like to live in Delhi! I did not want to be negative but the shock was hard! Once I got a little better, I tried to collect information about work in Delhi and visa requirements. I met with a kind woman, my husband's colleague, in charge of visa issues, and after looking at my business visa, she thought that I could work in India if I get a job offer either in power engineering or economics. However, she was not sure about the conditions under which it would happen. She promised to do some research by talking to some of her contacts in the central administration. She explained to me that rules kept changing and unless you talked to the right person, you might start off on the wrong path. She gave several examples of former colleagues who did not have the right visas upon entering India and they had to struggle to fix their situation. In most cases, the whole process had to be restarted from scratch. Entire families had to go back to the US to get the right visa type and nothing could be done locally.

A couple of days before our return, we also visited some apartments and houses for me to get a feel of the housing market. For the prices that were quoted and the relative condition of the properties, it was disheartening to think about leaving the US. I kept playing the same question in my mind: *Does God have a place for us in New Delhi?*

Out of the properties, we identified an apartment in one of the recommended colonies that had a ground floor and a basement. We thought it could be a good option and wanted to place an option to lease it from June 2008. We spoke to the logistics manager at my husband's office. He kindly offered to have the premises checked by one of his technicians before we committed ourselves to any deal. The housing market in Delhi was hot because of supply constraints, and a lot of expatriate staff were willing to compromise on quality to have at least a place to stay upon arrival. We had also heard of jungle-like commercial practices where the landlords allowed themselves a large discretion. The general rule was that until you got possession of the premises, you should expect anything—your lease could be cancelled because someone else had made a better offer after you signed, or the punch list items could not be addressed because if you did not want the property "as-is" someone else would. Having all of these peculiarities in mind, we took an appointment for the inspection. When we went to the place, the technician uncovered a lot of problems, the most significant one being some sewage water flowing into the basement, but it was nicely covered, unnoticeable to the novice. In Hindi, the technician got more information from the guard. In a matter of thirty minutes, he spotted so many defects and issues, in particular the sewage and mold problems in the basement. He advised us not to retain the place and we dropped it.

During this first trip, we could not find a conveniently located and suitable place to rent. My attraction to Delhi was over! My husband completed his professional mission and we took off to Washington, DC. For the first few days after our return, moving to India was simply out of question! I was having mixed feelings about the move, but the recent trip cleared them all! I was not going anywhere! My sisters laughed at me by mimicking my Indian dance moves I used to do before the trip.

CHAPTER ELEVEN

STRUGGLING TO FIT IN GOD'S PLAN: A BATTLE OF A DOUBTING CHRISTIAN HEART BUT STILL MOVING AS THE LORD PLANNED.

Fatimata and Kwawu

Fatimata: My first trip to New Delhi was a disaster. I started thinking about alternate arrangements. What would happen if my short trip experience was the norm during my stay in India? In my mind, we had to organize things better. My husband would go first, settle in, and once he was done, the kids and I would join him. I wanted him to go by himself and not drag me along into that country! I did not want to go to India! Once he had settled, I would manage later on to go and visit him with our children during their vacation. A lot of people had done it before, so why couldn't we?

My husband fought back that idea, which was completely unacceptable to him, as he had witnessed erosion in family ties over and over whenever such a situation was created. "Why would the Lord Jesus Christ of Nazareth take me to a place where I was not at all attracted to?" I kept asking myself. Why did I get so sick? Why was the trip so disappointing? Were my expectations of India too high?

My husband and I decided to reapply the proven principle: "no need to fight, continue to pray for clarity, and ask the Lord Jesus Christ to confirm the direction we had to take." After three to four weeks, we started talking about another visit to clear the first bad impressions. We agreed to embark on it with lower but clear expectations that we would examine all the pros and cons for this relocation. At that point in time, the only clear beneficiary of the entire process was my husband, and at the aggregate family level, the costs were quite high. We listed again all the points that we would review during the trip and agreed on a date. This time, my husband opted for a friendlier hotel: the Intercontinental Hotel at Connaught Place. He'd stayed during his previous trips in this hotel.

For this second trip, I again put my trust in the Lord and I praised Him for given me a second opportunity. The more I praised Him, the more I felt comfortable about going again to India. The planning was quite relaxed, the children were on Easter vacation, and they could spend time with family friends. We took off again from DC near the end of March. At arrival in New Delhi, I was more positive and ignored those who were staring at me. The air quality seemed much better and I did not have any breathing issues at the airport. I was relieved and felt more confident on our way to the hotel. Although not as famous as the Imperial Hotel, this hotel featured renovated rooms of modern design with new facilities. To my husband's delight, I liked this hotel much better. I did not have to face a group of beggars every time I stepped out of the hotel. Another positive feature of the hotel was the ethnically diverse breakfast buffet, which allowed me to sample quite a few dishes. This time, my husband devoted more time to our trip and common relocation issues, visiting apartments, going to the American Embassy School to start the registration process for the children, and meeting families with children and getting their advice about life in Delhi.

We again met with the nice woman who was in charge of the visa issues and she had positive news for us! The one-year business visa that I'd gotten for my first trip was unrestricted and I could work in any organization. Without doing anything, I was the first one ready to move to Delhi, as my husband still had to apply for the appropriate visa! What a paradox! The Lord works in mysterious ways: the person who was the most worried and reluctant was the first in line to move, at least on the administrative side. Was it enough to lower my guard? What if it was just a coincidence?

Kwawu: *Where would the family stay?*

This was a crucial question for which I, the leader of the family, could not yet produce an answer. It was pressing hard on us to find a place in the remaining five days of our joint trip so that my wife could be reassured that we were not leaving Washington, DC, without knowing where to land. She is of the type who wants to have everything clear-cut and ready. Since I was the one leading the family into this move, I had to at least deliver on the dwelling place front! The earlier both of us could settle on something that she liked, the better it would be for the family balance.

We restarted the apartment hunt and visited quite a few places having our preferred configuration of a ground floor and basement apartment. For most of these apartments, the basement was essentially a storage place, and they all had mold and watermarks on the walls. We were quite disappointed, but for the remaining two days of our stay, we visited three more of the same floor plan and in different colonies. Based on the recommendations of the administrative briefing document we were given at my office, we eliminated each and every one of them. We reviewed our stay and had to admit that we had not made any tangible progress. Here we were, at the end of our second joint trip, without having identified any place to stay. We prayed to the Lord, thanked Him for the guidance, restated our commitment and desire to follow His instructions, and left New Delhi in peace. Even though we did not find an apartment, we were confident that we would find one that would meet our family needs.

During our second trip, we also had the opportunity to work with another real-estate agent we were introduced to during our first joint trip. He was very capable and knowledgeable of both the Indian landlord's mind as well as the expatriate needs. Self-made man, he was also very astute in his negotiations. He was quite different from the other real-estate agents, working primarily for subsidiaries of well-established companies abroad. After a couple of visits, we were convinced that he was the guy we needed to help us navigate in the Delhi housing jungle. Although landlords were quoting horrendous prices for expatriates, he would always counteroffer with lower amounts (although still high compared to the quality of the properties). He explained that many organizations were not ready to pay hefty rental prices. He confessed that my organization was the only one capable of competing with the multinational corporations. He also confessed that he, like all real-estate agents, knew all the maximum rental prices (ceilings—highest amount each organization was willing to pay) for each type of family size and category of accommodation. Since he was a master in negotiations, we spent time discussing negotiation strategies and the market trends, especially whether the latest inflationary trends would sustain for a longer period. With him, we learned to decode quite a few things, and we refined a method to determine the equivalent rental price based on terms and conditions asked by the landlord. As said before, in New Delhi, the landlords had every right, and the prospective international tenants were at their whip. Your level of courtship and abdication depended on how badly you needed the accommodation.

We were crossing into April 2008 and our two joint trips were inconclusive. Out of all the apartments we visited, not a single ground floor and basement apartment was conveniently located and adequate enough for us to retain, but we spotted one apartment not yet finished in one of the colonies not too far from the Diplomatic Enclave. It was a first-floor apartment that had a functional design with proportionate spaces.

Back in Washington, we decided to give it more thought. It was not our preferred floor but it was the only one with decent and practical features. With what we knew about the quality of water and electricity in Delhi, the traffic and congestion problems, the pollution and safety issues, that apartment was the best compromise for all of us. Every member of the family could fit in it. Given its location, it would also allow us to go to one of the hospitals in Chanakya Puri serving the expatriate community in New Delhi. We decided to indicate to our dynamic real-estate agent that it was our preferred choice and that he should start the negotiation as soon as possible.

Fatimata: *Would the blessings of my second trip erase the disappointment of my first trip?*

By the Lord's grace, I was not ill during my second trip. We completed the registration process of our children, and I got the confirmation that I could work in New Delhi. All these positive elements contributed to bring the pendulum of the move on the right side. I was not as disappointed upon my return to Washington as I was after the first trip. Still, I hadn't totally bought into the whole idea! At the same time, I was convincing myself that we were in the plan of the Mighty One for our family, and I found it difficult to assuage the increasing doubts about this move to Delhi.

My husband was satisfied that we had at least identified an apartment, but to me, it was a remotely satisfactory choice. One day, on our way to work in Washington, DC, we were discussing the house-hunting process and how it appeared much complicated than anticipated. My husband tried to convince me to accept the provision of God, and he was hoping to hear me express the same cheerfulness about our prospective apartment. I was just not in the mood, and I derided our common choice and indicated to him that there was no reason for me to be happy about it. In my mental framework, I could not imagine that there was not one major sign that could confirm that we were led by the Almighty God. Finding a convenient apartment was at least one thing that should have indicated His mighty hands over this entire process. My husband tried to reassure me that he would not force me to go or live in a place where I would not be happy. He promised to look at more properties during his next trip, scheduled for May.

Kwawu: *Would you, Lord, finally lead us to a conveniently located and pleasant place?*

With my wife's health issues, I could not compromise on the place where we would live. She needed a safe place where she could retreat from the Delhi environment. The discussion in the car was really difficult, as I was thinking that we were nearing a happy outcome of our apartment search for me to focus on the other aspects of the relocation. Since my wife was not happy about the apartment, I crossed it off in my mind and prayed earnestly again that the Lord would lead us. This May trip was the last one before the summer move and I definitely needed to find a good and satisfactory dwelling place.

Everyone at my office in Washington, DC, and in New Delhi was showing concern about me not finding an apartment. What could

I do? The pressure was mounting, but I could not pretend I had a place. I spent the end of my May trip looking at all ground floor and basement options that I could find. Somehow, none of the very few options was adequate.

During that trip, our own agent showed the apartment we were interested in to another prospective tenant, who ended up taking it. Despite our interest and to our surprise, our agent was negotiating the same apartment for another of his clients. It was May 11, 2008, and to make us swallow the pill, the agent spontaneously informed me that he would be able to provide basic amenities in the apartment that we would eventually find while waiting for our shipment to arrive in India. I asked him to clarify and he confirmed that he could provide on a complimentary basis a refrigerator, a couple of beds with mattresses, a washing machine, a cooking range if needed, some utensils, an ensemble of sofas, chairs, a center table for the living room, and a dining table with six chairs.

We did not even have a place yet but we had already temporary furniture. I didn't know that such services were available in Delhi. He explained to me that he regularly provided such services to expatriates and he would be pleased to do so with us. As usual, I noted down everything in my small relocation notebook. The Lord worked in mysterious ways, and I thanked Him that at least a logistic problem was solved!

Finally, among the last options I visited, I started seriously thinking about one particular ground floor/basement apartment in the colony where we spotted the earlier first-floor apartment. I thought it could be an option. All in all, it had most of the features we were looking for, but I was not with my dear wife to confirm whether the choice was good or not. We had discovered long ago that for every major item, unless both of us agreed on it, a unilateral decision only led to a bad experience. Here I was, trying to decide for both. In the house search, our two pairs of eyes and two brains were better at screening.

So, I took a lot of pictures and sent them over by email, explaining the features of the prospective apartment, such as a visitor bathroom opening directly into the dining room, a kitchen layout carved out of the remaining space in the house, the master bedroom opening into a rear space (quite neglected) leading to a park, and the living room combined with the dining room, which was relatively small. However, since we had a large basement, I thought we could have the kids' playroom and entertainment space there. During the same period, another colleague was also undertaking his pre-assignment trip with his wife. They had also looked at the same apartment, but since they wanted a house at any rate, the apartment did not meet their needs. However, they thought it was a good option, and my mind settled on it. I couldn't have anticipated the turmoil we would go through.

A couple of days before I left, on May 13, 2008, I had the opportunity to meet the landlord, an old distinguished fellow with a good reputation, along with the logistics manager of my company. All throughout this house-hunting process, we had kept him in the loop as the final sounding board. The asking price was INR 4.25 laks per month (about US$10,000 eq.) with an escalation of 10 percent every year. This was way too high for the maximum rental allowance of 3.00 lakhs (about US$7,000 eq. per month), even if I would agree to pay a little extra out of my pocket. With my simulation model, we worked out a counteroffer close to the 3.25 lakhs per month (about US$7,600 eq.) with some stretched terms such as one-year rent advance payment and lock-in period for eighteen months at least, to remain within a reasonable bracket above my maximum rental allowance. All of these adjustments did not impress the landlord who held his apartment in high esteem and refused to engage. The meeting was over in a matter of ten minutes, and all the efforts and expectations were brought to nothing.

The real-estate agent later told me that the negotiation process could have succeeded if we were inclining to accept the landlord's conditions. For him, the fact that the latter came to the meeting was an indication that he was interested. I discussed with our agent a fallback strategy and agreed that we would continue to show interest, as well as maintain a regular contact with the landlord. According to the agent, a monthly rental price of 3.50 lakhs (about US$8,200 eq.) would have done the trick, but it would have meant an additional monthly expense of more than US$1,100 for the basic rent. On May 15, at five p.m., I met again the landlord before he traveled abroad for a month. His final offer was 3.40 lakhs (US$7,900 eq. per month) with an escalation of 10 percent after two years. I left Delhi disappointed but still trusting the Lord that somehow a solution could be found to our housing problem.

Fatimata: Packing our belongings and not knowing where to stay.

My husband desired to extend his trip to continue the negotiations with the owner's son, but we decided against it because it would have restricted our ability and limited the time we had to deal with the relocation process on the Washington end. The clock started ticking with a loud sound. We were already in the middle of May and our anticipated move was for the end of June 2008. We could not agree on a date of departure, but the actual relocation process had already begun with the survey of our items that took place a week before.

At this stage, several pieces of the puzzle were missing and it made us pray earnestly to the Lord Jesus Christ for guidance and wisdom in making decisions. How to manage expectations at the family level and put in place a decent fallback strategy? We prayed in tongues on several occasions, confident that all the pieces would fit together at the right time. The issues we had to handle at home were not obvious. What do we do with our house? Do we rent or sell it in a depressed market? What should we take and what should we leave? What about the car? All these questions were difficult, as things were not settled at our new destination.

The movers packed our items as scheduled in the second week of June. We selected the items based on the hope that the Lord would give us the apartment my husband had selected. We spent the rest of the month coordinating with the workers repairing the house while we were still in touch with our Delhi agent to monitor the negotiation process. We subsequently learned that the apartment had been on the market for quite some time, at least three months, because the landlord wanted a high rent and our agent advised us that after four months he would start tapering his expectations. Since the apartment was our only option we finally settled for it, although I did not see and could not figure out some of the floor plan details on the pictures. We continued to pray with fervor and in the Holy Spirit. At some point, we sealed the house in one accord, basing our faith on Matthew 18:18–19, "I tell you the truth, whatever you bind on earth will be bound in heaven, and whatever you loose on earth will be loosed in heaven. Again, I tell you that if two of you on earth agree about anything you ask for, it will be done for you by my Father in heaven." We asked the Lord Jesus Christ to reserve it for us, which essentially meant to keep it on the market but invisible to prospective tenants.

Fatimata: *A breakthrough or the beginning of trouble?*

On June 14, our agent called to inform us that the owner had finally accepted a rental price of INR 3.40 lakhs/month, starting from July 15, 2008, for three years and without any increase. We praised the

Lord for having opened a door! But with the limited experience and the rental stories we heard about, we could not shout victory until a letter of intent and a proper contract were signed, and, most importantly, we got into the place. The final price was still above our maximum rental allowance of 3 lakhs and we had to pay every month about US$1,100 out of our pocket, in addition to the housing deduction the institution would make every month to cover part of the rental costs. On June 17, we spoke again to our agent to confirm the details of his discussions with the owner, which he did on June 19, 2008. He also conveyed to us that he has shared the same information with the office logistics manager, including the requirements for a twelve-month advance rent payment, roughly US$90,000 and a start date of July 1, 2008.

Although excited that we finally got the owner's agreement, we were apprehensive about the house condition. With this rental price, we would have to take the apartment as-is without the possibility of asking for any repairs. From the agent's description, the apartment was not in proper condition and I started worrying again about the trouble that we might endure in such a situation. As we were in the midst of packing and shutting down our various activities and service contracts in Washington, DC, it was difficult to handle the administrative process at the Delhi end.

Fatimata: *Finally, a clear provision from the Lord Almighty . . .*

On June 19, 2008, another important development took place. During a discussion with the resource management department, my husband was informed that the office had increased the rental allowance for a family with two children to 4.25 lakhs per month (US$10,000 eq.), given the difficult housing market conditions. What a timely provision from the Lord! The office increased our rental allowance from US$7,000 to US$10,000. We now have enough resources to widen our apartment search. He called me to relay the information. We paused, thought about the goodness of the Lord, and thanked Him profusely for His provision.

A day later, on June 20, 2008, our agent informed us that he had to pay out of his pocket INR 50,000 (US$1,200 eq.) as earnest deposit to hold the apartment, with the full knowledge that my husband's organization did not encourage such practice, although very common in India. If it was true, the agent clearly went out of his way to take a risk, and knowing the Indian environment, we saw it as a way to bind us and the owner into a deal. We realized that we needed to continue this rental search process with our eyes wide open to avoid been trapped in a deal that would work against our interests.

Fatimata: When would the never-ending apartment search end?

We were reaching the end of our time in Washington, DC. We only had about two weeks left and we needed to secure this apartment before our flight, which was loosely scheduled for early July. During his last trip, my husband was able to open a bank account but no checkbook was issued to him. He wrote to the office logistics manager in Delhi to seek advice on how to handle the payment for the one-year rental advance. We discovered that nothing could be done because the administrative procedure was far too complex to handle from abroad. We called our agent on June 27 and discussed a couple of changes to the proposed contractual terms: the lease would start on July 15, but we would get possession of the apartment on July 8, the expected landing date in New Delhi, and suggested a couple of modifications in the apartment that we deemed important. The final rental price of INR 3.52 lakhs per month (a little more than US$8,200 per month) fit perfectly in our budget, and well below the maximum monthly rental allowance of INR 4.25 lakhs.

Given all the hurdles to reach this point, the agent took it upon himself to pay a higher token money as an earnest deposit to the owner. On July 1, 2008, at 12:46 EST, we finally concluded the epic search of an apartment in Delhi. We praised God that we also got the one for which we sent our belongings to Delhi. What a journey and what a victory over challenging circumstances! We rejoiced in the Lord and thanked Him again for His provision. Finally, the most important piece of the puzzle was in place, and we had five days before we took off. I was relieved, knowing that I would not spend time with my children in hotel rooms somewhere in Delhi!

In addition, without paying any money ourselves, we got the assurances that on arrival we could also move in with basic furniture provided by our agent. Prayer to the Almighty God, perseverance, and patience had paid off! Did the Bible not reassure us in Proverbs 16:3, "Commit your works to the LORD and your plans will be established," and in 1 Peter 5:7, "casting all your anxiety on Him, because He cares for you"? The months of anxiety and frustration were over, at least we thought, and we could now focus on the final activities before the take-off. Time was running out, but at least we knew we had a place! What a joyful and peaceful feeling.

CHAPTER TWELVE

A FAREWELL TO WASHINGTON, DC, AND LANDING IN NEW DELHI. ARE WE THERE YET? A STEP AT A TIME WITH THE LORD

Fatimata and Kwawu

Fatimata: We took off on July 6, 2008, with the kids and me trying to contain our sad feelings. It was overwhelming to bid good-bye to our friends and the children cried. After almost seven years in DC following our return from Paris, we were again on the road, this time heading to a difficult country. My husband did his best to cheer us up but the atmosphere was heavy. When we went to France, we had high expectations about the experience, we had a lot of friends and family members in the country, it was in close proximity to Africa, and it was a familiar environment. This time, the only assurance we had was that the Lord was leading us!

Fatimata: *How would the landing in New Delhi and India be?*

I was speechless during the first segment of the trip with still a lot of questions running through my mind. In London, during the transit, we were all exhausted and tried to take some rest. My husband checked his email account and sent a couple of emails to ensure that the welcoming team and cars would be at the airport. During the second part of the flight from London to Delhi, we tried to ignore the interrogative looks from our future neighbors and talked as much as possible about the upcoming experience. We finally arrived in New Delhi, tired, and the first hiccup occurred. The agent was not at the airport as agreed and he had not given the keys of the apartment to any of the welcoming drivers. My husband called up our agent but could not reach him. The tension was high—after more than three hours and a short trip to the Hyatt Hotel to see if we could get a day room, we finally got the keys and headed to the apartment.

When I got in, I went straight to the kitchen. The disappointment was profound. The kitchen was too small and the floor plan had little functionality. It was worse than I thought! What did I see in the pictures my husband had sent to me during his May 2008 trip? I understood better the angles and the available space. With one look at my face, my husband could easily see that I was not happy. He quickly moved to another part of the apartment. I contained my feelings as we conducted a survey of the apartment to see if things were according to the discussions with the owner and our agent. We discovered that it was not the case. The apartment had not been cleaned, nor did the owner fix anything we discussed. The amenities our agent promised to temporarily set in the apartment were not in place. What to do? Our son and daughter were crying, as they were tired, hungry, and disappointed by the apartment. Our first day in Delhi was not happy at all! The office driver took us out to a restaurant. The food was too spicy for the kids, although my husband and I enjoyed it very much. We had to wait again several hours for the apartment to be cleaned before we could get in. Our new life had just started, and there was no turning back!

Fatimata: *Are we there yet?*

Power cuts are frequent in New Delhi, especially in the summer. Unfortunately, there was no immediate start of the back-up generator whenever the power would go off. Surprise, surprise . . . the back-up generator was not even working nor had not even worked in a long time because it did not belong to the owner. The air-conditioners were not serviced or maintained as per the negotiations, nor were the various water heaters and other circuits in the apartment. Living in that apartment was a source of major discomfort. Although I tried to maintain my calm, my patience was running thin.

My husband would leave the apartment in the morning with the promise to come back as soon as possible. He would only show up late in the afternoon with a smile on his face, and enquire about our well-being. I felt the days were longer as the heat in the apartment was making it uncomfortable. The air-conditioners did not work properly. On top of all, I could not cook the food we all wanted and the children were finding it difficult to play outside, especially my son who could not tolerate the strong smells. Although I tried hard, I did not like the floor plan, and the apartment was not convenient from my point of view. But, since I knew how we got in, I would praise the Lord confessing that He never made mistakes. Washington was behind us and the Lord had brought us to this place . . . in His wisdom! I shifted my focus from the daily annoyance and tried to provide the best support I could to my husband and our children.

Since we had landed as a team, we were resolute to continue as a team led by the Most High in this unknown land. We tried to resolve the apartment issues while working to finalize the contractual documents. There was a standard contract to be signed, and since we had the letter of intent, we thought the process would be straightforward. But the owner was coming up with new terms and conditions at every occasion. Where were we heading? There were so many confusing signals! However, we were in peace, knowing that the Lord had brought us to that apartment.

On July 30, 2008, the entire family, including the children, went to a conciliatory meeting with the office lawyer. Since we were getting exhausted by these unusual circumstances, we accepted many clauses and provisions against our interests as tenants. The lawyer subsequently told us that he would prepare a new draft contract/lease for us to review by August 1, 2008, which would reflect the agreed changes. When we came back from that meeting, we felt ripped off by a coalition of people who cooked a deal in Hindi and imposed it on us. What could we have done differently? We were praying about finalizing this contract as soon as possible to move on with furnishing the apartment to our taste and settle. It was that simple, but it was simply impossible!

That night, after the meeting, we knelt and prayed about the situation. The story of Pharaoh and the Israelites in Exodus came to our mind, and as we were reflecting about it, the Lord gave us a word of wisdom. If indeed, it was His will for us to stay in the apartment, this final settlement would be acceptable to the Owner since the contractual terms were clearly in his favor.

The next day, we did not get a draft contract from the lawyer. Instead, the owner came up with new terms. A 35 or 40 percent rent increase would take place after the initial three-year period. We would have to give a six-month notice period for vacating the said premises after two and a half years of the lease period. A special damage clause was added in case we did not hand over vacant said premises at the time of expiry of the lease or its earlier termination, and a common arbitrator would have to be appointed. What was he so afraid about? All of a sudden, this basic rental contract had become an international contract, and it was so apparent that our foreign status was at play here. Why were we subject to undue frustrations in this foreign land? Were we being abused simply because we were different? We tried to understand the reasons behind that change of attitude but could not find a single one that was satisfactory. Working for a reputable international organization was not even enough to allay the concerns of this owner. All the assurances given by the office lawyer were not enough. What were they up to? Only the Lord knew! We returned to our routine of praying earnestly and in the Holy Spirit. We tried to focus on other aspects of our relocation.

These recurrent power cuts were making the apartment uncomfortable. I would call my husband at the office whenever an attempt to address the situation myself was not successful. I was regularly experiencing a breathing discomfort, and at times, it was as if I was about to have an asthma attack. Although we had reduced our eating out, I was still having several abdominal pains, which made the adjustment even harder. With all the problems in the apartment, the four of us ended up sleeping in one room and only using one bathroom. It was our security perimeter! We later understood that the previous tenant was single and we figured out that the room we all retreated to might have been his. It was difficult to imagine that the owner would consider his four-bedroom apartment to be a jewel. To us, the picture was clear. The Lord brought us there for a purpose and we knew that we had to stay in that apartment. We were also convinced that we should not bow to any of the pressures, holding on this well-known verse of Romans 8:31: "If God is for us, who can be against us?" We kept our confession that the same God who brought us in would open the door for us to get out, without any problems. We decided to wisely fight the inconsistencies of our interlocutors. Since we wrote down every significant event or milestone and managed to attend all key meetings, it was easy to spot the untruths or attempts to mislead us. From the glitches of early August, we decided to systematically triangulate all the information received and asked for clarification until satisfied. The disagreement with the owner was growing larger. The Lord was on our side, and our agent, contrary to what we had experienced so far, was enlisted to defend our interests and his. Having paid the token money of INR 125,000 (about US$3,000 eq.) out of his pocket, not concluding this deal or us walking out of it would have meant a net loss for him. We reassured him that he would get his money back and we just needed him to extend his full cooperation. The theory of convergence of interests was at play again. To better handle the matters, we adopted a two-step negotiation process: I would go first to discuss, we would review the information collected, and if needed, my husband would step in the discussion to convey our final position. The owner started to show his impatience. Although defaulting on most of the terms of the Letter of Intent, he started asking for his one-year advance payment without even signing the contract. In our minds' eye, it was absolutely impossible to make the payment of US$90,000.

Kwawu: *Is it a door opened by the Lord for us?*

The tension was escalating. I felt sorry for the adjustment pains of my wife and children, but there was nothing I could immediately do to alleviate them. But the Lord was working on an exit plan for us. On August 18, 2008, the owner and his son met us at the apartment. They explained that we were getting the premises at a discounted rental price because of the ongoing construction next door, and that if we were not pleased with the proposed rental terms and conditions (reflective of market practices), we were free to vacate the premises. They also told us that we had three options: a short-term rental for a couple of months, with penalty clauses for delay in vacation, a one-year lease, which could not work, or a three-year lease under the owner's impossible conditions. They were just throwing us out of the apartment.

That night, we let them rant and did not say a word as we were reminded of Proverbs 14:17, "A quick-tempered man acts foolishly, and a man of evil devices is hated," and of James 1:19, "This you know, my beloved brethren. But everyone must be quick to hear, slow to speak and slow to anger." We promised to think about our options and come back to them. We prayed about the situation again and asked the Lord for direction. The owner had clearly opened the door for us, but was it enough to walk out of these negotiations? In our opinion, another act was needed as recommended in Deuteronomy 19:15: "One witness is not enough to convict a man accused of any crime or offense he may have committed. A matter must be established by the testimony of two or three witnesses." Not having an immediate fallback solution, we were in the mood of negotiating a four-month short-term lease and conveyed it to the owner's son. We also agreed to let prospective tenants visit the apartment at mutually convenient and agreed times.

On August 21, the owner's wife called my wife to inform her that some prospective tenants would be visiting the apartment and that instructions should be given to the maid accordingly. My wife raised the issue of the timing of the visits and the answer was another rant. She clearly stated that she did not care about us. She just wanted to find a good tenant for her house. It was now clear to us that we could no longer stay in this apartment. We wanted a place to settle but not at all costs. Our children were already affected by this difficult transition, and having people visiting the house every day would add additional frustrations. We went to see the office logistics manager to learn more about our options, and during the discussions, it became clearer that we needed to make hard decisions. The only viable option was to vacate the apartment as soon as we could. We were really downcast and at the same time relieved. We thought this couple of medical doctors, distinguished in appearance and having lived abroad, would be our landlords, and we would have a fantastic relationship. But it was not their intention and we could not afford to live in fear since the Lord commanded us in Deuteronomy 31:6 to "Be strong and of good courage, do not fear nor be afraid of them; for the LORD your God, He is the One who goes with you. He will not leave you nor forsake you."

Fatimata: *Are we ready to move out after less than two months and where would we stay?*

We were stranded! Fortunately, by the Lord's grace, we had only purchased small items. The container with our belongings from Washington was still on its way. Things had started off on the bad side. Despite all the turmoil we were going through, one thing remained: the peace of the Almighty Lord, which was overflowing. We knew that our Almighty Father could not have made a mistake. What a paradox! In the midst of the storm, our heart was at peace!

My husband remembered an email sent to him about a new service apartment in Saket (the suburbs of Delhi) and introductory rates were ending on August 31, 2008. He pulled it out and started making calls. By the Lord's grace, apartments were still available and we decided to visit the place. With the additional information collected from the office administration, we now had to make a choice between two or three service apartments at various distances from our main interest centers.

At the end of the school day for the children, we decided to visit the service apartments before making a decision. We made the arrangement to start with the first one, the nearest to the office and the kids' school. Somehow, it took us more than forty-five minutes to reach the place and the attendant was not very friendly. As we were leaving, we saw a building across the street where a group of people was carrying a body enrolled in a mat and heading inside. A brilliant light shone on us: it was a crematory, and the sequence of events and circumstances was amazing. In a discussion the day before, we came to know about crematories, but thought they were outside the colonies or neighborhoods. On our way to a place where we were supposed to live temporarily, we encountered a group heading to the nearby crematory . . . all of this when we had to make a decision. Whether close or not to the office or the kids' school, that place was ruled out. We did not want to live in a place knowing that dead bodies were being burned every day nearby.

We headed out to the second place, and the road was packed with cars. The children drew our attention to the peculiar scenes on the sidewalks—cows searching garbage cans, tents with naked kids and mothers looking after them—and our children were not accustomed to seeing such things. After an hour drive, we reached the place. We visited the apartment-hotel in the Saket mall and after negotiations with the commercial director, we settled for one unit. The location and convenience of the place was right in line with what we could expect in New Delhi, so we didn't even bother visiting the third apartment. We spent an hour and a half on our way back and thought that the commute would be difficult on a daily basis. But we did not have the choice; at least we would have a temporary relief for one or two months, as we embarked on a new house-hunting exercise.

CHAPTER THIRTEEN

TRUSTING WITHOUT UNDERSTANDING: THE MOVE FROM OUR NEW DELHI APARTMENT TO A HOTEL. A DOOR CLOSES AND ANOTHER ONE OPENS!

Fatimata

On August 26, we wrote a letter to the owner providing the reasons and a date for vacating his apartment. The real-estate agent had given it to the owner, but the owner refused to acknowledge receipt. On a subsequent letter, dated September 1, 2008, we forwarded him the check for the time spent in his apartment, with the token money deducted and reimbursed to the agent. We were free at last. For more than 104 days, from May 13 to August 26, 2008, we could not reach any agreement to the satisfaction of the owner, despite having compromised significantly on many terms and conditions.

The Retreat (from the apartment to the hotel): A simple coincidence or the providence of the Lord? Can the Lord Jesus Christ bless us beyond measure as He said in the Bible?

Two things happened during the negotiations for the suite in the Svelte Hotel. With the new maximum rental allowance, we were able to afford a grand suite—two separate bedrooms (one for the children and one for the parents), plus a small open kitchen to the living room, and we agreed to an initial duration of two months. We were happy with the unit and just praised our mighty God for such a provision. It was clearly an upgrade compared to our one-bedroom, one-bathroom security zone! In addition, the hotel was very close to another of the recommended specialty hospitals, which was a clear plus.

During our second visit, the hotel director, a woman with a generous heart, stated that she loved our family and decided to upgrade us. We were given the presidential suite number 601. It was the only presidential suite in the apartment-hotel. Without the lady with a generous heart, we would not have been able to afford it. What a dramatic change from an apartment that had many flaws to a place where we could finally have some rest. We did not have to care about house maintenance, cleaning products, changing sheets, and other chores. We were treated to a continental breakfast every morning and had a laundry daily allowance of two pieces of clothes. All of a sudden, the pains of dealing with a greedy landlord were behind us and thinking about all these unfortunate events,[14] we blessed the Lord that He had brought us to a place[15] where He could restore us and heal our wounds. These events brought our family life to another level. We were happy to be together, enjoying quality time. We only had one car, and since it took us forty-five to sixty minutes

---

[14] "Behold, I give unto you power to tread on serpents and scorpions, and over all the power of the enemy: and nothing shall by any means hurt you. Notwithstanding in this rejoice not, that the spirits are subject unto you; but rather rejoice, because your names are written in heaven" (Luke 10:19–20).

[15] "But a Samaritan, as he traveled, came where the man was; and when he saw him, he took pity on him. He went to him and bandaged his wounds, pouring on oil and wine. Then he put the man on his own donkey, took him to an inn and took care of him. The next day he took out two silver coins and gave them to the innkeeper. 'Look after him,' he said, 'and when I return, I will reimburse you for any extra expense you may have'" (Luke 10:33–35).

in the morning from the apartment-hotel to the American Embassy School, and about one-and-a-half- to two-and-a-half hours in the afternoon to go back, we ended up commuting together. We would share stories and read the Bible, and discuss life issues in Delhi and try to draw lessons from them. In the hotel, whenever we were not satisfied, we knew whom to call and the issue was quickly resolved. The hotel had a swimming pool on its terrace and a lifeguard on duty. Since it was still summer, we would go up but the kids could not fully enjoy it because they did not know how to swim. I asked the hotel director about the possibility of giving swimming lessons to the kids and to my surprise she gave instructions to the lifeguards to be the kids' swimming instructors free of charge.

"There is a time for everything", according to the Ecclesiastes 3:1, and the Lord's time is always the best.

When we concluded the deal on our initial apartment, we discussed spending a couple of nights in a wonderful hotel before moving into the apartment. The idea was to give a short vacation to our son and daughter since the move did not allow us to plan anything for them that year. We did not pursue the idea, as my husband was eager to settle quickly in New Delhi and have his daily routine established before the start of the school year in early August. God turned things upside down and offered us a better plan. We were worried about our children being affected by this transition and were sorry we could not take care of them as we would have liked. But the Lord also had them in mind when allowing us to go through this difficult settlement. After all the troubles, we were now in a presidential suite with great comfort and the children had free private swimming lessons after school. The Lord said in Isaiah 55:8–9, "'For my thoughts are not your thoughts, neither are your ways my ways,' declares the LORD. 'As the heavens are higher than the earth, so are my ways higher than your ways and my thoughts than your thoughts.'"

One month went by quickly, and despite our best efforts, we could not find an adequate place. We were now working with several real-estate agents, but we quickly discovered that the choices were limited and the agent we had for our initial apartment was the best. We again adopted a two-step strategy: my husband would go first with the realtor and if he considered an option to be worth the trouble, I would join him for the visit. At the hotel, people were asking us about the move-out date and we did not have an answer, and we were reaching the end of our initial contract period. We extended for another month with the option of giving a two-day notice to vacate the presidential suite if we found a place. People were getting concerned at the office that we had not settled, but it was not because we were not trying. We could not tell our parents back in Africa and in the US that the landing went wayward and that we were looking for another place. It would have raised their anxiety level for nothing. We were in the hands of the Lord, under His feathers,[16] and it was sufficient for us since He had displayed so many wonders and encouraged us in so many ways.

After some time, the kids lost interest in finding a dwelling place, I thought it was a waste of time, but my husband kept on. To increase our success rate and avoid being captured by one agent, we would discuss several options at the same time—one option only through one agent to avoid any confusion. Places were coming up and going on the market because people were willing to pay cash to help the owner avoid paying taxes and sign a contract with lower rental amounts. But nothing seemed to be working out for us! According to many Indians, "The stars were not aligned for us." How could we explain that our Lord was in control?

---

[16] "Even though I walk through the valley of the shadow of death, I will fear no evil, for you are with me; your rod and your staff, they comfort me" (Psalm 23:4).

One apartment we were interested in and negotiating through our agent was clearly overpriced. The owner was expecting a rental price of 6.5 lakhs (a little more than US$16,400 eq.) per month for a four-bedroom apartment and a basement. This option was better than the previous one we vacated and had been on the market already for more than three months. With the unfolding economic and financial crises, the pressure on the housing market was cooling off, and the influx of expatriates was decreasing.

One day, in the cafeteria, one of my husband's colleagues told him that he also went to visit the place we were interested in but it was small for his family. That day, we discovered that our agent, who had advised not to tell anyone that we were interested to avoid complications in the negotiation process, was actually showing it to others and even negotiating it for them. My husband immediately called to inform me about the situation and we agreed to call the agent to let him know that we did not like his attitude.

On November 18, we had a difficult conversation with our realtor. We realized he was playing every possible trick to take advantage of our condition. During the night we reconsidered our options and decided to pray about the situation. We asked the Lord Jesus Christ to show us the path to consider. We clearly indicated to the Lord that He could deliver us from the wickedness of our interlocutors by creating a direct contact with the landlord. On November 19, we plowed through our daily routines not knowing what to expect. But we kept on trusting the Lord for His intervention. For sure, the apartment had gone from 6.5 (US$16,400 eq.) to 5.5 to 5.0 and we were at 4.25 lakh (about US$10,000 eq.), according to the last indication from the realtor. My husband continued to visit places that came on the market to make sure that something was not left out in our daily struggle.

Who could have imagined that we would escape the terrorist attacks in Mumbai so narrowly?

As we were approaching Thanksgiving break, Kwawu told his colleagues that he would not go on a business trip to Mumbai. The reason was simple: he wanted and needed to celebrate Thanksgiving with his family. This was one of our favorite times of the year in the US. The year had been hectic up to that point and spending time to reflect and thank the Lord Almighty for His goodness was appropriate for the family. Little did we know that it was the Lord's way to preserve the family from the trauma of the Mumbai terrorist attacks.[17] My husband would have been in one of the attacked hotels, as some of his colleagues were, if he had gone on that trip. I was shocked at the thought that my husband's life would have been at stake had he decided to go with his colleagues.

We spent the day praising God for His goodness, and thanking Him for having created the conditions for us to remain together as a family, far away from the turmoil of these vicious attacks. We watched the attack on TV, followed what was branded by the Indian media as "The September 11" of India. We were in the Washington, DC area in a hotel near the Pentagon on September 11, 2001 when the brutal attacks occurred, and we witnessed the turmoil, having just returned from France. Here we were again on November 26, 2008, trying to settle in India and witnessing another terrorist attack. The Bible declares in Psalm 91 that "Whoever dwells in the shelter

---

[17] The Mumbai terrorist attacks happened on November 26, 2008. On that day, my husband's entire team was on mission in Mumbai. While some members were able to quickly return to Delhi, others did not have that grace. At least two of them were trapped in the hotels that were under attack. By the Lord's grace, they escaped without physical injury after many hours trapped in their hotel rooms. What an ordeal!

of the Most High will rest in the shadow of the Almighty." We were happy to be under His protection[18] and to count on His care.

We began the month of December 2008 with mixed feelings. It was taking too long for us to find a place. Even the not-so-good opportunities were beyond our reach for one reason or the other. We had at least six to eight real-estate agents, hoping that we would line up an apartment. We now understood the market rules, we knew how to structure a contract with multiple variables, and we were experts in price simulations and negotiations, but there was nothing, at the horizon.

Sealing another apartment in prayer: was it the right one for us?

On December 8, 2008, the tension in our presidential suite was palpable as we were struggling to maintain our focus. We again prayed the Lord for our apartment, committing our ways to the Lord and telling Him how much we were counting on Him to lead us to a safe shore. That was the only way we could pray in our situation. We shared Philippians 4:6–7, "Do not be anxious about anything, but in every situation, by prayer and petition, with thanksgiving, present your requests to God. And the peace of God, which transcends all understanding, will guard your hearts and your minds in Christ Jesus," and we took off for the day. Counting on the Lord was not easy, but it was the sure path! Since we had told our children to pray for an apartment, we decided to take them with us to visit the apartment we were negotiating on. We arrived shortly before five o'clock. We were welcomed by a strident noise of birds, which lasted for about fifteen minutes. We asked the guard if it was usual. He

---

[18] "The LORD is your keeper; the LORD is your shade on your right hand. The sun shall not strike you by day, nor the moon by night. The LORD will keep you from all evil; he will keep your life. The LORD will keep your going out and your coming in from this time forth and forevermore" (Psalm 121:5–8 ESV).

responded with an affirmative gesture and conveyed with a smile—as my daughter started covering her ears—that it also happened around five in the morning.

We proceeded with the visit, and to our surprise, the children were not happy about the apartment. As they were going through the various rooms and the curious floor plan, they even doubted our sanity. I was really disappointed on two accounts: first, the kids' comments hit the nail and were delivered with a small dose of sarcasm, and second, contrary to what the real-estate agent conveyed to us, the apartment needed significant repair and maintenance. It was closed for quite some time, the spider webs were all over, and several large mold spots were apparent in the basement. To conclude the negotiations and have the repairs done would take another two months in the Indian context and we did not have much patience left. We probably visited all the existing and possible ground floor/ basement options in the colonies of Delhi we were interested in.

That night, we had two trains of thought: if God was leading our search, what have we done wrong or where have we lost the light? And second, since my husband did not stop his search when the negotiations for the potential apartment started, he did not feel that we needed to worry. In his mind, we had done our best, and there must have been a purpose to this rollercoaster search. Recounting our blessings—the presidential suite, the continental breakfast, a car and a pretty reliable driver, and life going on at a decent pace amid my health issues. We were convinced that we would finally land, but when and how? There was no answer. Although I was not as convinced as my husband was, I tried to remember all that the Lord had done for us and knew He would do it again!

After talking to our various realtors, I agreed to go for anything decent available in the upper floors and trusted the Lord that the frequent power cuts in Delhi would not lead to a great inconvenience. Even by widening our search criteria, we could not reach a closure in our apartment search. I was so disappointed with the outcome of our apartment search that I told my husband I would take any apartment on the market if an owner agreed. I just wanted to settle although the hotel was very convenient. Our children needed to have a place to call home and to run and play with their friends, which was not the case at the hotel.

Are we about to find a new apartment? Should we stay to finalize the paperwork or go on winter break?

To curb our frustration, Kwawu decided to continue the house search by himself, mostly during the weekends, and if he lined up something worth a second look, he would bring in the "jury." We spotted another convenient flat on the third floor, and after two parental rounds with the realtor, we took the kids to visit. As my daughter was entering the apartment, which had an entrance on the ground floor and a large open staircase to the third floor as well as an elevator, she started shouting that she did not feel secure. My daughter was crying and begging us not to rent this apartment. What happened to her? Should we move on despite this unusual reaction from my daughter? We reassured her that we would not take any apartment where she would not feel comfortable. With the assurances given by the realtor, we were hoping to hear from the owner, but by the end of the second quarter of the school year, around December 18, we did not have anything concrete. In anticipation of a sudden resolution, my husband prepared the draft contractual documents based on the samples we had reviewed again and again. Our plans to spend the winter break settling in our new apartment were on the brink of being shattered. My husband was holding on to the idea of a positive development, but there was no traction in the family.

CHAPTER FOURTEEN

A WINTER BREAK RELIEF, NEW FACET OF OUR HOST COUNTRY, AND STILL TAKING BABY STEPS WITH THE LORD.

Fatimata and Kwawu

Fatimata: We were all tired of the unending search and not at all enthusiastic over the prospects of spending Christmas in New Delhi. We did not plan anything because of this house search. On December 20, 2008, a heated discussion happened between our two children, and I on one side and my husband and his convictions on the other side. The kids and I didn't want to stay in New Delhi and the decision was final. On December 21, we started making arrangements to travel to the US for the rest of the winter break and we finalized our flight reservations for December 23, 2008. We frantically packed our luggage and did some last minute shopping, headed to the airport, looking forward to our return.

That day, we discovered another facet of our host country. By such an unthinkable combination of facts, my husband's visa had expired. His diplomatic ID card was not considered a valid residency document at the airport. How could a country prevent him from going out of it with a valid diplomatic ID card? It was the first time I witnessed this type of situation. Despite all the reasons conveyed in good faith, my husband was not allowed to board the plane, being considered an illegal alien. The agent who dealt with us was rather rude and he refused to help us out. The issue was escalated to his supervisor, but we got the same response. Here we were, the kids crying on one side, myself upset on the other and refusing to leave on vacation without my husband. I wondered if India was at all fun and if our stay there had any purpose. We were eliciting the curiosity of the airport customs staff. What could we do with the plane waiting for us? The airline staff was waiting for us to make up our minds. The airport customs staff was advising me and the children to board the plane and leave my husband behind. Neither the kids nor I wanted to leave their dad behind. My normally calm son was so upset that night that he filled out two suggestion cards for the airport authorities. My daughter was begging the officers to let her father travel with her. None of the family members' supplications helped. Things got even worse: my husband was simply disembarked. And the rest of the family followed suit. That night, December 23, 2008 was a bad one!

We came back to our hotel around 4:30 a.m., exhausted mentally and physically. Neither my husband nor I could sleep thinking about all the implications—the biggest one of having to spend the entire Christmas break in Delhi with a family that was not happy! Early in the morning, my husband prayed with fervor and headed out to the office. With the advice of the woman responsible for the visa processing, he prepared all the required documents and waited earnestly for her arrival.

With her skillful maneuvering, she managed to get my husband's visa extended without any delay, as well as those of the children, which were about to expire. She instructed the travel agent to rebook the family on the flight leaving on December 24, which happened to have enough free seats to accommodate the entire family! What a joy! What a relief! Favor from above and a mighty intervention since it was December 23, two days before Christmas, and by such a skillful design, everything was lined up for our departure! We spent the rest of the day thinking about the whole experience and recognizing how blessed we were to have a Father in heaven!

There we were again, ready to fly!

When we showed up at the airport that evening, most of the immigration police agents, who were witnesses of the early morning incident, were openly surprised to see us, the entire family, back on the same day and ready to board. The agent who took our passports asked my husband if he were a Nigerian. He also asked him, "Why were you not allowed on the plane? Were you illegal?" To which my husband replied, "That is what your colleagues said." We finally boarded and for the first time in so many months, we were pleased to be on our way out.

Incredible India did not take six months to wear the family down mentally, and I was clearly out of strength as the plane took off. My son and daughter were happily looking forward to seeing their friends and cousins back in the US.

We spent the vacation in the US discussing the entire experience in India, re-assessing our relocation strategy, myself leaning forcefully toward staying behind with the kids, and my husband going back alone. My husband was not into that scheme. Whenever he thought about that eventuality, he was not comfortable with the idea and he clearly expressed it. I was running away because it was just too hard! I knew that the move was from the Lord, but it was just too hard to live in India. For me to stay in the US was not the direction we wanted to take as a family nor what we sensed was the Lord's direction. Weighing all options, an additional source of stress to our family life was the least we needed. For many reasons, our return to

India was delayed until late January 2009. We just decided to make the best for our stay. It was as if I was rediscovering all the good parts of the US, the courtesy of people, life without too much trouble, and the many opportunities. You enjoy something more after you have lost it! I thank the Lord for having brought us back to the US.

Kwawu: After the Christmas break, we came back to Delhi with renewed energy, refreshed feelings, and a desire to live day by day, focusing on the positive aspects of our relocation. We were still in our presidential suite with all its amenities, our driver was still willing to work for us, and things were going well for me on the professional front.

For my wife, the story was still very mixed, as she was clearly struggling to adjust to a different, rough environment. Health-wise, in the first six months of our coming to India, she had five painful episodes of intestinal problems. The scariest one was when she could not even drink water, the pain being so excruciating. She thought she could handle it and the pain would subside, but it didn't. She was crying, and there was nothing I could do to help. None of the stomach medications at hand was helping. I had to take her to a doctor recommended by the British Embassy. As soon as he saw her, he suspected an episode of tourista and he prescribed several types of medication, including one to reduce the pain. When he heard about the corticotherapy, he felt sorry for her and advised her to go to one well-known hospital with an experienced endocrinologist. He was of the view that my wife could not survive in the Indian environment unless she was closely monitored.

On the respiratory front, she had a couple of instances of real discomfort and we went to see a pneumologist in the nearby specialty hospital. He reviewed her medical history and suggested that she tried a new medicine that was recently introduced in India for allergy and asthma problems. When he gave the name, we told him that she had been on that medication three years ago in the US but it did not produce any good results. Because we believed that God was leading us here, we just thought that she would be fine. At her work in an Indian energy research company, she was finding it difficult to blend in. She was experiencing the same Hindi-induced isolation that I was going through but in her case there was no minimal possibility to correct the situation.

Kwawu: *Were we ready for the mighty intervention of God?*

On the house-hunting front, we restarted our search, albeit without much enthusiasm and hope, with our group of realtors. The financial crisis that hit the US in November 2008 was starting to spread and various multinational companies were affected. Many executives relocated out of the normal seasons, and suddenly, the housing market started its downward transition. Two things worked in our favor with the downturn in the market—more properties were becoming available and owners started to soften their negotiation positions and expanding their choices of tenants.

One day, while I was on a business trip out of town, a realtor had taken my wife to visit a second-floor terrace apartment, which she very much liked. The floor plan was adequate, and she told me that peace gushed into her heart as she entered the apartment. Of course, since she was not heavily involved in the search process, she did not have any particular reference. I asked her the address of the apartment. All of a sudden, memories started gushing out as I realized it was the top floor in the same building of the first-floor apartment we had let go. What a coincidence! I told my wife that it was simply unbelievable that it was the apartment she'd like, and I reminded her about the discussion we had back in May 2008. Wow, what was going on, Lord?

When I returned to New Delhi, I went the following Saturday to visit the apartment with my wife, and confirmed that it was indeed the same floor plan as the first-floor apartment. I recalled that at the time I had visited, the second floor was already taken and I was told that the rental price was 4.5 lakhs (more than US$10,500 eq.). The same day, we visited another house at Anand Niketan, another nearby colony. The kids liked the house because it was a split floor, with mini steps between the various parts, and the lower floor offered several options to play "hide and seek." This time, at least with the downturn in the market, we had stronger winds under our wings. In the process, my wife was clearly inclined to go for the second floor, but somehow, I still wanted the Anand Niketan house to successfully conclude. I remembered the soft voice of the Lord telling me that I was resisting His will! We set up another visit with the owner of the Anand Niketan house, during which I had the curious idea to ask him to switch on all the lights in the living room. As soon as he did it, something exploded and the entire set of lights switched off. It was not possible to get them back on. For us, the decision was clear. The Lord had just showed us that we were heading for trouble if we chose the house.

We drove back to the other colony and concluded the negotiations with the owner. And the price was within our budget! On our way back to the hotel, we thought a lot about our Indian journey so far and how the Lord had led us to this apartment . . . in a convoluted circle. It was already March 2009, and we needed to move out of the apartment-hotel quickly. Little did we know that it was not over yet!

With an apartment in view, we started looking forward to the day we would leave the presidential suite. We were already six months into our search, but there were a couple of issues that needed to be sorted out. The owner could not come to a firm decision and he started playing games. Having lived in India for some time now, we were adamant not to move ahead with the apartment without having a clear lease agreement signed with no ambiguities. Our shipment of June 2008, which had arrived in December 2008, was still in the storage, and we were about to pay extra storage and insurance charges. But we refused to be distracted by that constraint and cried out to the Lord Jesus Christ for help and guidance. The discussions lingered for another month and finally victory broke in. We moved into the apartment at the request of the owner who did not want to incur further rental losses. However, we did not release the payment of the first month until the issues were properly sorted out.

Finally, seven months after the negative experience with our first landlord, we were able to secure a new apartment. We could once again give an address to our friends and family abroad. What a blessing from the Lord! As said in Proverb 13:19a, "A longing fulfilled is sweet to the soul." In addition, a relocation allowance that was withheld because we did not have a place to live was paid out with a 30 percent bonus since the local currency had devaluated by 30 percent between the time we landed and the time we moved into the apartment. Moreover, the exchange rate of the dollar to the rupee was the highest and it had not reached that again the entire time we were living in India. What a blessing!

CHAPTER FIFTEEN

A ROLLERCOASTER OF SOCIAL AND HEALTH ADJUSTMENT: PAINFUL FOR THE FLESH BUT SPIRIT IN PEACE! TRUSTING DAILY THE LORD ALMIGHTY.

Kwawu and Fatimata

Kwawu: Working was becoming increasingly complicated for my wife and the joy of her partnership flattened. Struggling to find balance between the new environment and her values, she spent more and more time praying for God's direction. In a matter of days, the Lord closed the door after we settled in our new apartment. At that time, we sincerely thought we would now have a peaceful life in Delhi and go about our business, as originally intended. We took the opportunity to throw a big party for our daughter's birthday to thank the Lord for His goodness and mercy. Both the apartment and the top terrace were nicely decorated. We set up indoor games, as well as hired a group of young Christians that were in the entertainment sector. They were organizing themes birthday parties to support charities and pay for their studies. My wife even managed to find an elephant as a ride for the guests. It was such a relief to finally have a place we could call home. The children could now enjoy their games and have friends over. That bliss did not last for a very long time because we discovered another facet of the life in Delhi.

Fatimata: "Take heart when you go through different tribulations" (John 16:33).

Having an apartment that I liked and where I was free to move around brought me a lot of joy. Finally, I could cook when I wanted to. I could have friends over. Looking back, I was so grateful that the Lord brought us into this apartment. As mentioned, traffic was so hectic and driving so difficult in New Delhi that hiring a local driver was mandatory. Regular cleaning was also required to prevent accumulation of dust and dirt, and we needed household help now that we were no longer in the apartment hotel. We tried to treat our driver and household staff nicely but it was misinterpreted. The nicer we were, the more disappointed we ended up being. We lost the driver we had during the transition after he had an episode of heavy drinking, fighting with the guards, and threatening to harm the family. This happened without any warning signs. We learned later on that our driver had been heavily drinking and smoking and using spices to dissipate the odor, all this while driving us for more than six months. God had protected us even when we didn't know it. From that day forward, we couldn't seem to have both a reliable driver and a trusted housemaid at the same time. When we thought we had a reliable driver, our housemaid would leave, and when we had a good housemaid, we could not keep our driver. Somehow, the pieces could not fit together no matter what, and as a consequence, we were praying about our stay in India, offering praises and giving thanks[19] to the Lord that He would lead us through.

---

[19] "Give thanks in all circumstances, for this is God's will for you in Christ Jesus" (1 Thessalonians 5:18).

CHAPTER SIXTEEN

THE DECLINE OF FATIMATA'S HEALTH

Kwawu

We called on the Lord continuously and prayed repeatedly in the Holy Spirit. It was the only way for us to overcome these unusual circumstances as we were also struggling with my wife's failing health.

Despite all of our efforts—having air-conditioners and purifiers operating continually, cooking with all precautious and boiling everything possible—my wife was going through a difficult period and our family life was under stress. My wife's health was deteriorating with these nagging intestinal problems. We were extremely cautious, selecting the best quality food, washing food with hot water, cooking it with the utmost hygiene, and my wife taking vitamin supplements to strengthen her immune system. But progress was difficult to perceive; although we tried very hard, some days were better than others, but the general trend was a downward spiral to a greater weakness. Amazingly, her respiratory problems were reducing and she was able to gradually reduce her dose of oral corticosteroids. Starting from 10 mg a day when we arrived, she was able to reduce it to 7.5 mg a day and her asthma was still under control. What was at play here? We could not understand. We were worried about asthma and pollution, but something else was throwing our fight into another direction.

Day by day, I saw my wife's strength dwindling and her abdominal pains growing. Our trips to the pharmacy or to the hospital were not enough to ease the pains. After our return from the 2009 Christmas holiday in the US, things became even more difficult in January 2010 when chronic diarrhea set in. Despite the regular antibiotic treatments, neither the chronic abdominal pains nor the symptoms of infection went away. Every day was a struggle to lead a normal life. We would pray, ask God for strength and healing, focus on the positive signs . . . a little more strength one day, a reduced diarrhea frequency on another one (eight visits to the bathroom instead of ten before 7:50 a.m., soft deliveries instead of pure liquid releases, etc.) and surrender every situation into His hands.[20] Despite all of that, my wife was losing weight at a steady rate; her hands started to ache, and she could not hold anything or exert any pressure to open a bottle, for instance. She would wake up in the middle of the night, in pain and in tears, and the only thing I could do was to pray. Having been sick in the past, she did not want to end up in a hospital again, and in extreme cases, I would take her to the emergency room with the hope that somehow a reasonable explanation would be given to all her stubborn symptoms. Her vital signs would be checked, and after a round of observations, the treatment would be "rest, antibiotics, pain-relief medicine for the stomach, and if symptoms continue, come back to see us." She would spend most of the time between the couch and the bathroom, and she could not do any activity with the kids.

On the house front, stability was a remote concept. But on the professional side, I was happy with my work, and challenges in the Indian energy sector were really fascinating. I was the only

---

[20] "Do not be anxious about anything, but in every situation, by prayer and petition, with thanksgiving, present your requests to God. And the peace of God, which transcends all understanding, will guard your hearts and your minds in Christ Jesus" (Philippians 4:6–7).

happy person in the household, and the question came back again of splitting the family, with me staying behind and my wife and children returning to the US. To that thought, I opposed the same resistance but this time, it was apparent that something really wrong was unfolding. What would happen if in my obstinacy something irreversible happened to my dear wife? What would I tell my children? That I loved my job so much that I failed to attend to their mother's needs?

It was in the midst of those thoughts that I went on a business trip to Bangladesh. I ended up in a situation where I could not decline going abroad. Several senior people had already declined and if I had to do the same things, the level of representation at the workshop on gender and energy would not have been adequate.

The day I was leaving, my wife was in tears and in pain. Over the past week, the situation had been out of control. In the middle of the night, she almost fainted because of the tenacious pains. Leaving her behind and trusting her to the care of our ten-year old daughter and almost twelve-year old son was the only thing I could afford at that time. The only other thing was to trust the entire family to the care of our Heavenly and Almighty Father to lead us through such circumstances.

I boarded the plane with so many mixed feelings and I started to think deeply about continuing this assignment, which I liked very much. Was it really worth it to sacrifice my wife and the sanity of my family because I wanted to continue to enjoy my professional life? The answer was not an easy one, and I would just pray that God would lead us to the right decision. After delivering my parts of the seminar, all these questions rushed through my mind. I wished that I would go back to Delhi and witness a mighty deliverance from the Lord!

I changed my return plans, and in Kolkata (West Bengal) I consulted my emails while in transit. There was a letter, as open and honest as it could be, from my wife that said, "I have sustained so much for you, and I hope you are not going to let me die in Delhi because of your professional career!" That email hit several chords, and I remembered the promise I had made before we embarked as a family on this Indian journey. I boarded the plane in Kolkata with the clear knowledge that we were hitting a wall!

After rejecting the idea of a split, in my mind, I just realized that a family split could be the answer! How egotistic or selfish would that idea be after more than thirteen years of marriage and struggles of every kind? All of a sudden, for my career, I was leaning toward an idea that I refused to entertain for so long! She dropped the prospects of her brilliant future as the first female power engineer of Burkina Faso to follow me to the US. When she was almost settled professionally, I uprooted her to go to Paris because of the golden opportunity to work at a leading investment bank. When she regained her professional ground in the US, we went to Delhi, despite all of her reluctance and genuine reasons. Now, at this juncture, after she had been through so much, I would just drop her back to the US because I wanted to enjoy another year of being the lead energy specialist for India. The thought was really tempting! But I could not hold it for a very long time.

The moment I stepped into our apartment, the discussion started again. What were we going to do? For her, it was clear that there was no way she would continue in Delhi. She was losing energy by the second without any remedy. Whenever she would eat, her stomach would inflate like a balloon and remained bloated for several hours. It would eventually shrink and leave her totally drained.

One of my work colleagues gave me the name of a reputed gastroenterologist to have a second opinion. We went to see him right away. After listening to all her symptoms, he gave us several disease options and indicated that he needed to do more tests to arrive at a proper diagnostic. The hygienic conditions at that hospital were not the best we had encountered in Delhi, and with the recent experience of one of our colleagues losing her husband in one of the reputable hospitals in the city I asked whether I could attend the various exams. The answer was a clear-cut no! How were we going to ensure that no mistakes were made in this Delhi hospital? How could we minimize the risk of internal damages during the various exploration exams that were scheduled under general anesthesia? How could we trust the medical staff when my delicate wife required so much more attention and had special needs? These questions made the decision process even more complicated, but after a long, hard look, only one option stood out among the multiple combinations: we had to move out of Delhi as a family and no other alternative seemed viable!

The last question to resolve was how to break the news to my management. Just before I went to Bangladesh, I met the HR focal point of my department in the most unusual circumstance. He came to Delhi for a short visit and as he was going walking through the hallway looking for someone else, he ended up in my office. To his question about how things were going, I responded that I was really happy about my assignment but there was one stubborn issue that we were not able to address. My wife was constantly ill but all the treatments were simply ineffective. At the time of that exchange, I had not yet made any decision, and I thought I could start my administrative request from there. I tried to reach out to that HR colleague in DC but it was impossible. He was very busy attending many meetings. So I decided to send an email to my immediate supervisor, with a copy to his supervisor[21] and the HR colleague, to seek his approval to depart. I was ready for any outcome, but I was resolved to press on, as my thought process was complete and the difficult decision had already been made.

---

[21] "If you see the poor oppressed in a district, and justice and rights denied, do not be surprised at such things; for one official is eyed by a higher one, and over them both are others higher still" (Ecclesiastes 5:8).

CHAPTER SEVENTEEN

TAKE-OFF FROM INDIA: STILL PRAISING THE LORD WITH A STRONG FAITH!

Kwawu

As one could imagine, several exchanges took place, but we were confident before the Lord that we made the right decision. A couple of days later, I even got an email from my manager on my birthday announcing my immediate replacement, despite my expressed willingness to continue the assignment under other suitable arrangement. I found the terms of the letter without compassion. Why did I receive such letter on my birthday? I wondered why the Lord Jesus Christ allowed such a disappointing thing. In the transition, it seemed that we were hit from all sides.

But our focus was on how to organize the return to the US. We were clearly unprepared to move out of Delhi at that time. When we were making our relocation plans to Delhi, we were prepared to complete three years and possibly a fourth year. This major change took us by surprise and we asked the Lord to guide[22] us step by step. There were several issues to take care of in a really short amount of time. We needed to get all the paperwork ready for the academic transfer

---

[22] "Commit to the LORD whatever you do, and your plans will succeed" (Proverbs 16:3).

of the children when their school was on vacation; we needed to ask for the reimbursement of the US$4,000 school deposit, which as per the school regulations was non-reimbursable; we needed to sell our nineteen-month old car in the context of the Indian administrative procedures and regulations; and we needed find a place to stay in the Washington area.

After assessing all options, we decided to focus on securing admission into the old private school the children had attended, which had so well prepared them for their academic life in Delhi. Having a school in mind simplified our equations, and we needed to focus on finding a transition arrangement to ease our relocation to the DC area. The school in Delhi was closed and the teachers were on holiday until early August. We could not start collecting the various information and letters of recommendation from the teachers. We could not seek a reimbursement of our deposit of $4,000 because it was a guarantor of the seats for the kids for the upcoming academic year. We prayed about the situation and sent a letter explaining our circumstances. We attached my birthday gift letter that my manager sent regarding my decision to leave. The terms of the "gift letter" were so convincing that I got the full refund of the US$4,000 deposit! Unbelievable! The birthday gift was indeed a sweet one, but at that time, I did not know it. We later used the same gift letter as a supporting document to a mortgage application to buy a house in the Washington, DC, area. Given the sub-prime crisis in the US, the lending institution wanted an official document from my employer that would certify that the house would serve as our primary residence. Again, the terms of the "gift letter" were so convincing that the mortgage officer was satisfied, without any reservation! Amazing providence!

We needed to sell our car and we discovered that the process was lengthy and uncertain because we had not completed our three-year stay. Based on Indian diplomatic regulations, we had to sell the car to a diplomat, who had to secure official permission to buy our car for which we needed to have permission to sell. The intricate process was mind-boggling. We could not sell our own car without official permission! All of a sudden, having bought a new car turned out to be a bad decision. We could not export the car to another country in Africa, we could not take the car with us to the US, we could not give the car to whomever we could think of, and we could not sell the car! At the same time, a colleague of ours, who also had to leave prematurely for medical reasons, had to store his car and pay storage charges after his departure because the administrative hurdle was not resolved. We ended up praying about that situation, hoping that the Lord would give us a breakthrough.

We had to travel to the US to plan for our return, but we could not do it with our children because it would be a short, intense, and busy trip. There was no way we could entrust our children to the care of our household help. We needed a responsible adult. Fortunately, several months before, some friends from France—a medical doctor and his wife, a pharmacist—had planned to visit us with their two children during the month of August. Since the school year in Delhi started in early August, we were convinced that the presence of their kids would make it difficult for our children to focus on their homework and the curriculum. We were a little reluctant to have them over but assessing the pros and cons, we decided to accommodate[23] them and make their program in such a way that the disturbance for our children would be minimal. Little did we know that the presence of our friends would give us the peace of mind required to travel to the US for a short period of time. My wife was confident that with a doctor and a pharmacist, every urgent health need of the children would be taken care of. In addition, because we traveled to the US,

---

[23] "So in everything, do to others what you would have them do to you, for this sums up the Law and the Prophets" (Matthew 7:12).

our friends were able to really discover Delhi and organize their stay with much latitude than if we were there. Who could have imagined such a perfect plan?[24]

Wearing a pullover in the heat of Delhi summer? What a paradox!

We were struggling to see how we could organize our trip to DC to minimize the toll on my wife's already weak health. The journey to DC was long, and we tried to allow her to get as much rest as possible before the trip, despite the frantic preparations. On our way to the airport, she was not feeling well but she was hopeful that the Lord would sustain her. We did not know that something else was unfolding. Drawing from the experience we had when we moved to Delhi, we decided to take our winter clothes with us and take them to DC during the pre-assignment visit. We packed our clothes and luggage and checked the weight of our five bags before leaving home. They were properly balanced and within the authorized limits.

When we arrived at the Delhi airport, we decided to recheck the luggage and wrapped them with plastic for extra protection. However, the luggage handler tricked us into believing that our bags were not properly balanced and were overweight. We trusted him, reshuffled our luggage, and put some of the extra kilos in our carry-on luggage. We were left with pullovers that were dear to us and we could not set them aside. So we decided to take them as extra clothes.

It was above one hundred and four degrees Farenheit in Delhi, in the middle of August, and we laughed at ourselves that in the heat of Delhi, we could take thick wool pullovers. When we reached the check-in counters, we got upgraded from economy to business

---

[24] "The men were amazed and asked, 'What kind of man is this? Even the winds and the waves obey him!'" (Matthew 8:7).

class on the Delhi to Paris segment. What a happy surprise! We were exhausted by all the preparations of this trip and having the possibility to travel in better conditions was really welcome. But we were not at the end of our surprises.

Somehow, when we got into the business-class cabin, it was freezing cold. The flight attendants tried hard to regulate the temperature in the cabin but to no avail. It was so freezing that some of the passengers required additional blankets but in our case, we had our heavy wool pullovers. We put them on and slept like babies! We were amazed at how God could organize the circumstances to meet our basic needs in such an unpredictable way! When we arrived in Paris, we were in better shape and ready to continue our relocation preparations. Thinking about all the uncertainties ahead, this episode of the wool pullovers in the Delhi summer was our constant reminder that God would prevail in our difficult circumstances. "Are not five sparrows sold for two pennies? Yet not one of them is forgotten by God. Indeed, the very hairs of your head are all numbered. Don't be afraid; you are worth more than many sparrows" (Luke 12:6–7). We completed our trip to DC, came back exhausted but grateful for the assistance and guidance from the Lord.

Three issues were now clearly on the table: the sale of the car, the move logistics, and the organization of the last days in Delhi as a family. The equations were not simple. We kept praying to the Lord and some of the answers came from the constraints previously set by Him. The move logistics were not easy to handle because we did not have a clear idea about what to leave behind and what to take to the US. Based on the survey done by the moving company, we were exceeding the freight allocation, so we had to carefully decide what to carry with us by plane and what to put in the container. Based on the US packing approach, it would not have been possible to carry our belongings but based on the Indian packing approach, we were able to put everything we had planned for in the container. The moving crew's team leader was very ingenious, and he managed to stuff our furniture with soft items, to the point where we had empty space in the container.

The process of selling the car ended the day we were leaving the country, and we handed the keys to the new owner at the end of the working day, just some hours before we went to the airport. Here again, the Lord intervened in an amazing way! We found a buyer who trusted us to transfer the money of the sale into our US account before the deal was complete. Until the last minute, we had the car under our responsibility and the buyer could not ask us to hand it over to him because the paperwork was still pending. The other interesting fact was that the Indian authorities had given the authorization just in time to allow us to sell our car, and this opened the door for those colleagues, who were stuck in the queue, to also complete their sale. After we left Delhi, the exception rule under which we could sell our car was revoked and new rules were put in place. We knew we owed this perfect timing to our Father's loving care. I remember we were rejoicing and at the same time discovering in real time that indeed He had everything under His sovereign control!

The entire family left India on August 31, 2010. Looking back, we realized that the two years we spent in Delhi were the most frightening, challenging, and special in our family life as we discovered another facet of God's grace and His loving care beyond measure. On all accounts, we were in heavy waters and at times, we thought we would be swallowed by the waves and strong winds. But He was watching over us, covering us with His mighty wings.[25]

---

[25] "They wandered from nation to nation, from one kingdom to another. He allowed no one to oppress them; for their sake he rebuked kings: Do not touch my anointed ones; do my prophets no harm" (Psalm 105:13–15).

We learned to pray resolutely for our enemies and authorities per the instructions of the Apostle Paul to Timothy:

> "First of all, then, I admonish and urge that petitions, prayers, intercessions, and thanksgivings be offered on behalf of all men, For kings and all who are in positions of authority or high responsibility, that we may pass a quiet and undisturbed life, a peaceable one in all godliness and reverence and seriousness in every way. For such is good and right, and pleasing and acceptable to God our savior for there is one God and one Mediator between God and men, the Man Christ Jesus, who gave Himself as a ransom for all, a fact attested to at the right and proper time."

Our landing to DC was smoother given that we had been in tougher places and we had learned to trust God daily! We started right away with doctor visits, exams, and treatments, but we still had questions with no answer. We were still in a dark cloud—hard pressed on all sides—but under His mighty wings. Nobody could tell us what would happen next, but God knows! He takes care of us and He will prevail! Amen.